"Need to say goodbye to the past? Need a fresh perspective on your present? You need the *hope* in these pages! You will be more courageous and you will see how living *now* will change your future."

Gregory L. Jantz, PhD, founder,
The Center • A Place for HOPE

"Love the book! Dr. Westfall has laid out a winning formula for vibrant living that draws on the experience of counseling thousands of folks . . . combined with sage advice from theological and mental health experts."

Jake Moe, cofounder, *Powder* magazine

"As a family doctor treating thousands of patients over thirty years, I have come to realize the inevitable truth: all of us struggle with our past, our failures, our regrets, and our shame. Not moving forward is the seed of depression and anxiety. We become stuck. Westfall offers a mountain of experience with sage advice entwined with wit and biblical texts. He has us reexamine the concepts of positive and negative thinking patterns, giving a benefit and risk analysis of each mindset. He humbly exposes the futility of personal misery, blaming others, and focusing on past trauma by relating his own stories. Finally, he gives us five poignant and enlightening steps toward what he terms as 'planning your past.' I recommend this read for anyone who is entrenched in the past but looking to move forward while reading insightful advice, enjoying humorous anecdotes, and discovering biblically based solutions."

David Spiro, MD

Live
Like There's No
Yesterday

BOOKS BY JOHN F. WESTFALL

Getting Past What You'll Never Get Over

I Didn't Sign Up for This

Coloring Outside the Lines

Enough Is Enough: Grace for the Restless Heart

Live

Like There's No

Yesterday

Discover the Freedom
of Leaving the Past Behind

JOHN F.
WESTFALL

Revell

a division of Baker Publishing Group
Grand Rapids, Michigan

Published by Revell
a division of Baker Publishing Group
PO Box 6287, Grand Rapids, MI 49516-6287
www.revellbooks.com

Printed in the United States of America

Library of Congress Cataloging-in-Publication Data
Names: Westfall, John, author.
Title: Live like there's no yesterday : discover the freedom of leaving the past behind / John F. Westfall.
Description: Grand Rapids, Michigan : Revell, a division of Baker Publishing Group, [2021] | Includes bibliographical references.
Identifiers: LCCN 2020056423 | ISBN 9780800740733 (casebound) | ISBN 9780800728083 (paperback)
Subjects: LCSH: Christian life. | Change (Psychology)—Religious aspects—Christianity. | Regret—Religious aspects—Christianity. | Attitude (Psychology)—Religious aspects—Christianity. | Thought and thinking—Religious aspects—Christianity.
Classification: LCC BV4509.5 .W43375 2021 | DDC 248.4—dc23
LC record available at https://lccn.loc.gov/2020056423

To protect the privacy of those who have shared their stories with the author, some details and names have been changed.

21 22 23 24 25 26 27   7 6 5 4 3 2 1

In keeping with biblical principles of creation stewardship, Baker Publishing Group advocates the responsible use of our natural resources. As a member of the Green Press Initiative, our company uses recycled paper when possible. The text paper of this book is composed in part of post-consumer waste.

This book is dedicated to the memory of my friend Jane Knickerbocker. She loomed large in our family, where she was called Auntie Mame. A lifetime of abuse, trauma, depression, and anxiety couldn't squelch her love of Jesus and her passion to nurture and encourage those who struggled both in faith and in life. I believe she was the most honest, negative optimist I've ever known.

Contents

Acknowledgments

Writing may sometimes feel like a lonely exercise, but I'm very aware that I'm never alone. I'm grateful for the many friends who have hung in with me through the ages and stages of life. Thank you for sharing the gift of your stories, wisdom, and encouragement.

Whether in printed words or unspoken influence, Eileen Westfall has lived most of this book over the fifty years we have been married. In addition to having the same birthday, we have also shared a lifetime of joy and sorrow, sickness and health, and richer and poorer. Since we were labeled the couple least likely to stay married one year, I guess we proved them wrong.

Damian Westfall, our son, has kept pushing me to not give up writing and living. He is a prolific author and a courageous trauma survivor, as well as a researcher for this book. I'm proud of him and grateful to be his dad.

I'm grateful for the input and help of David Pardee, John Langham, Pam Proske, Bob Marlowe, Gary Winkelman, David Meharg, Sheila and Walt Gustafson, Daniel Castillo, Diane Rocha, and David Doherty.

I'm also thankful for the insight and assistance of Rachel McRae, who guided me with her gentle persistence and editing skills at Revell Books.

What If There Was No Yesterday?

It's no use going back to yesterday, because I was a different person then. — Lewis Carroll

The sign on the hallway wall said, "Live Like There's No To-morrow!" I could hardly resist the urge to pull out a marking pen, cross out the word *Tomorrow*, and scribble under it "Yesterday!" I don't even remember what made me almost turn into an older version of an urban tagger, spraying graffiti and messages on our city walls. That afternoon I managed to control my impulse, but it got me thinking about what could happen if we learned to live like there's no yesterday.

Letting Go of Looking Back

Tomorrow was never much of an issue for me. I didn't worry or feel anxious about what was just up ahead. I wouldn't even know how to regret the future, since I hadn't messed it up yet. In fact, I rather liked the idea of the future because I'd get a fresh start. I guess I just didn't want to live like there was no tomorrow. Anyway, if today was all we had, and there wasn't going to be a tomorrow, I didn't know where hope would come from.

Yesterday, on the other hand, is definitely something I could live without. There have been times I dwelled in the past or looked back with both longing and regret. Sometimes the past haunted me, held me, or defined, limited, and frustrated me. Of course, the past also held victories, celebrations, and happy memories. But it seemed like I needed to dig around to find them in the pile of broken dreams and hurt feelings.

If our goal is to live each day with freedom and joy, we have a chance to learn from our past experiences without allowing them to interfere with the happiness and confidence that come from living intentionally today.

A lot has been said, thought, written, and sung about yesterday. After all, according to the Beatles, isn't it a place where all our troubles appear to be far away? If so, why wouldn't we want to dwell in the past?

I've probably spent way too much time looking over my shoulder, ruminating on things that have happened, or didn't happen, in my past. It's not like I mean to do it, but those yesterdays creep up on me and pretty soon the memories that get rekindled start burning bright, and it's hard to turn away.

Dwelling in the past isn't limited to recalling painful, negative experiences or memories. We can also focus on good things, celebrations, past experiences, and achievements, and even though they're positive, they can still keep us from experiencing the joy and freedom of today.

14

As a kid in Sunday school, I heard one Bible story that scared the stew out of me. It was the account of Abraham's relative Lot, who is told to take his family and flee their home before an impending disaster. They were warned not to look back as they ran for their lives to the nearby mountains. Everything was going along well, we were told, until we hit the verse, "But Lot's wife looked back, and she became a pillar of salt" (Gen. 19:26). I certainly had no desire to become a pillar of salt, much less a shaker or even a pinch of salt, so I spent my childhood trying not to get caught looking back.

Perhaps I was more like Lot's wife than I thought, because in spite of my childish sense of dread, I spent much of my life looking in proverbial rearview mirrors, remembering and ruminating on yesterday. Isn't it part of our human nature to see a "Wet Paint" sign and instinctively reach out to touch the paint to test if it's really wet? Is it even possible to hear the words "Don't turn around" without immediately turning to see why we aren't supposed to look back?

The Bible gives some pretty clear direction when it comes to how we deal with yesterday: "Forget the former things; do not dwell on the past" (Isa. 43:18). I admit it would be so much easier if I just did what that verse tells us to do.

Part of my problem might be that even after accepting the implications of that verse, and intentionally choosing to do as it says, I get bogged down—because right away I start thinking about the past in order to grasp what things are most important for me to forget. Like trying not to think of pink elephants, I end up dwelling on the past even as I try not to let it cross my mind.

There is no end to the books, articles, TED Talks, sermons, and blogs encouraging us to focus on the now and forget about the past. You'd think with all this learned and well-intentioned encouragement to live in the moment, we wouldn't have a problem. After all, how hard can it be to not look back, especially if, like me, you fear becoming a pillar of salt?

Of course, we all have our yesterdays. We carry with us lots of memorabilia, including happy memories, flashes of pain, carefully protected celebrations, and even a few trophies of failure. Pretending we have no past and denying our previous experiences doesn't solve anything; it just makes us seem a little creepy.

We can, however, live *like* there's no yesterday. As we come to understand how our previous experiences impact and often shape who we are today, we then can choose to act and react *intentionally* rather than automatically.

Corrective Lenses

Sometimes it can be hard to experience positive growth or change in our lives because we get stuck in a mire of memories and interactions that make it difficult to see ourselves and our situations with fresh clarity. It's as if our emotional vision and our spiritual vision get blurry.

I've worn glasses most of my life simply because I need them to see beyond about two feet in front of me. I'm nearsighted. This means I can read or do tasks that are close up, but anything very far away is just a big blur to me. Of course, my glasses help correct the problem and give me the ability to see things that are more distant.

Once, while I was leading a group on a tour in Hawaii, we arrived in Honolulu and checked into our hotel, and I immediately ran across the street to the beach at Waikiki. It was a beautiful afternoon and I couldn't wait to try body surfing in that sparkling water. Because I can't see very well without my glasses, I thought it best to wear them out into the ocean. Suddenly I was hit from behind by a crashing wave, and my glasses flew off into the water. I never found them. I tried diving down and swimming along the sandy shore, which was an exercise in futility because, as you might guess, without my glasses I couldn't see well enough to find them.

So here I was, the guide for a whole group of people, and I couldn't see a thing. I was functionally blind for the whole week, unable to see anything farther away than the length of my arm, pretending everything was fine so they'd never know what an idiot I was, swimming out into the ocean waves wearing my only pair of glasses.

This same misfortune can happen to us emotionally and spiritually. We are going along and something hits us from behind, catching us off guard. Often we are hit by a tough difficulty that is painful. We lose what may have helped us keep our focus, and now we can't see clearly or even understand what we are facing in our lives. It is hard to know what to pay attention to because it's all a blur.

Like my physical nearsightedness, we can find ourselves showing symptoms of emotional and relational nearsightedness as well. One of the indicators of this is our tendency to focus on things that are up close and immediate but lose sight of the bigger picture. We look at our immediate situations, losses, struggles, and unmet needs. But we can't focus on a broader vision that puts everything in perspective.

Sometimes I think it would be much better if we had something like glasses for our hearts or our minds. Imagine how freeing it would be to see our emotions and heartbreaks through the lenses of clarity and perspective. Likewise, we could process the memories, regrets, and resentments of the past in such a way that we could have a broad perspective of their impact on our lives today and in the future.

I've come to see that there is something that does work like a pair of glasses for our minds and hearts. It is the lens of thankfulness, which allows us to look up from our limited focus and see a bigger picture of our lives today and our hope for tomorrow. In the Psalms we are encouraged to "enter his gates with thanksgiving and his courts with praise; give thanks to him" (Ps. 100:4).

It's easy to become distracted by all the burdens, betrayals, successes, and failures from the past we carry with us every day. In time we become worn down, losing perspective and not feeling freedom or joy. But when we choose to be thankful in the midst of our troubles and frustrations, we begin a healing process that helps us live beyond our past.

"Do not be anxious about anything," Paul writes, "but in every situation . . . *with thanksgiving*, present your requests to God. And the peace of God, which transcends all understanding, will guard your hearts and your minds in Christ Jesus" (Phil. 4:6–7, emphasis mine). When we acknowledge and express thankfulness, we are able to see situations and people in fresh ways. Gratitude is the antidote for so many of our distressing thoughts and bitter feelings.

When we look at life through the perspective of thankfulness, it becomes easier to see and experience God's love. This in turn leads to freedom. It's exhilarating to have freedom that releases us from the fears that grip us, the regrets that gnaw at us, or the hurts and scars that trigger our traumas. We can be free to let go of the past that haunts and inhibits us in many ways.

When we choose to let go of the past, with all the resentment, shame, and memories of abuse it brings, we are free to live each day with confidence and hope. Choosing to let go is not the same as denying what may have happened, nor does it suggest it won't take time and effort to let it go in a healthy way. We won't forget, but we can forgive. In releasing the past, we release ourselves. When we forgive, the person who is most impacted is ourselves.

In *The Lion King*, Simba discusses with Rafiki, the shaman, his need to go back to his homeland and face his foes.

"Change is good," Rafiki counsels Simba.

"Yeah, but it's not easy," Simba responds. "I know what I have to do, but going back means I'll have to face my past. I've been running from it for so long."

Suddenly his friend smacks him in the head with a stick.

"Ow, what did you do that for?"

"It doesn't matter, it's in the past."

"Yeah, but it still hurts!"

"Yes, the past can hurt," responds Rafiki, "but the way I see it, you can either run from it or learn from it."[1]

What is true for Simba the lion is also true for us. Even if the past hurts, we can learn from it and move forward freely. Imagine a life where the past has no power to define or limit you. Nor can it wound or shame you. You can live free today because it's the past; it doesn't matter.

2

Fuhgeddaboudit! There's No Future in the Past

I've got my faults, but living in the past isn't one of them. There's no future in it. — Sparky Anderson, Major League Baseball Manager

I never watched *The Sopranos* throughout the years it was an award-winning television series. But once when I was home-bound while recovering from surgery, I got so bored I decided to binge-watch the whole thing from the beginning. I didn't make it all the way, because somewhere in season four I gave up on Tony Soprano and his mobster dealings and the killing of what seemed like the entire Italian-American community of New Jersey.

All was not lost, however, because I learned one of the most important terms ever mumbled: *fuhgeddaboudit*! I'm coming to realize this word has nearly universal application and seems appropriate for practically every situation.

Someone does something to help you; you thank them and they reply, "Fuhgeddaboudit." Or you let someone down and hurt them—you apologize and they say, "Fuhgeddaboudit." Perhaps someone owes you a great debt they can't repay. What are you going to do? Kill them and dump their body in the river? Well, perhaps, or you could just say, "Fuhgeddaboudit."

Fuhgeddaboudit becomes an expression of grace, a gift we don't deserve and could never earn, but which we definitely need.

I was surprised, watching *The Sopranos*, that in a world stuffed to the brim with cheating, lying, conniving, and murder, a ray of grace broke in to display forgiveness, generosity, mercy, and perhaps even love.

So, I say, "Fuhgeddaboudit!" Whatever others have done to us, said to us, done to hurt us, or owe us, there is a choice we can make. We can carry the hurt and resentment through our lives, distorting our present experiences and poisoning the future, or we can say, "Fuhgeddaboudit."

Finding Focus

"But one thing I do: Forgetting what is behind and straining toward what is ahead, I press on toward the goal" (Phil. 3:13–14). Paul wrote this to the early Christians so that they could move their focus from the past to their future as followers of Jesus. He compared himself to a runner in a race to illustrate his mindset and the motivation of his spiritual life. Like a runner, he needs to focus on his goal. He won't be successful if he doesn't concentrate on the race or if he's torn between competing goals that may distract or confuse him.

A runner must also focus on the next steps toward their goal. Paul implies that his spiritual life is similar, so he will not look back on his past steps or mistakes, but will instead keep his mind on improving each next step in the race until the goal is achieved. We too can learn from the past, but we aren't bound by things we have done or not done. We can determine how much of our past will affect us now. We also determine what aspects of our past we will let shape our attitudes and actions. The past has no power to do anything—unless we give it the power.

Unfortunately, most of us haven't learned to leave the past behind. Our thoughts are filled with ideas, reflections, and memories that can define us, limit us, and wreak havoc on our current situations and relationships by triggering old wounds, emotions, and loss.

Too often in counseling settings, a couple will be arguing or fighting about something and will resort to weaponizing their past hurts in order to inflict pain on each other. It's as if they are hoisting up a big garbage can of hurt and debris and dumping the whole mess on the other person's head. Usually the painful memories have a ring of truth, and the feelings are real, but over the years, the memories have evolved to the point where, though we are certain of their accuracy, they in fact are clouded and changed from the original event.

When we say we need to leave the past behind, what does it mean? Some think by simply not thinking about it, we become instantly free and able to live confidently and happily. But closing our minds to past experiences, relationships, problems, and failures will never make us free or happy. It just covers them up so they can continually sabotage our lives.

Instead of denial, we can bring our mistakes and hurts into the light where we can openly explore the dynamics of our lives to this point then respond appropriately to the situations. If we need to forgive ourselves, or someone else, then we do it. If we need to learn from an experience in order to respond differently when faced with a similar issue, then we explore the lessons that can be taken from it. We can't pretend something didn't happen or tell ourselves everything is fine when it's not.

We should avoid assuming we know why things happened the way they did, or why people treated us a certain way, or why we did what we did. These assumptions are usually wrong, because we are looking at the circumstances through distorted thinking. Rather than assume, it is sometimes possible to check reality. Often we can test our opinions and see if we are right. Even if we come up with many possible reasons, we still won't know for certain.

It's all right to recognize we may never know for certain why things happened the way they did. It's okay. After examining the experience, we can still choose to move on in a healthy way.

Letting Go

One of the things that connects all of us is our ability to experience pain. It doesn't matter if the pain is physical or emotional; we all have been hurt from time to time. Part of what makes us unique is how we deal with the pain.

"The purpose of life is not freedom from pain," writes Bruce Larson.

> If you have enough money to hire medical folks to keep you comatose, drugged and fed intravenously, you could live the rest of your life without ever having to feel pain. But that's hardly living. The purpose of life, according to Jesus, is to love God

24

with your whole heart, soul, mind and strength and to love your neighbors as yourself. That means loving a world full of people who are desperate for love, starting in your home or your neighborhood. Do that and you will experience pain. I promise! Look for a minute at this problem of pain from God's point of view. If God had wanted to avoid pain, there would be no people. We've been a problem ever since the Garden of Eden. We've been rejecting Him, betraying Him, ignoring Him. We've been a pain in the neck to God. And if God was unable to accept pain there'd be no relationship possible with His creation. There'd be no redemption. Why should we be any different?[1]

When emotional pain keeps us from healing from an experience, it is a sign that we aren't moving forward in a healthy, growing way. When we get stuck thinking about a painful situation and what should have happened, in our opinion, we risk becoming immobilized in painful memories and experiences.

Although we all have elements of the past that are upsetting and often debilitating, we are the people we are because of (or in spite of) our childhood, parents, education, and events we experienced. We can replace cynicism with intentional gratitude. This will help free us from our natural tendency to assume the worst or lock our minds into negative attitudes that form. We avoid thinking things like, *No one will ever love me again*, or *I'll never get hired again*. These types of ultimate conclusions set us up to wrap ourselves in defeat and block our ability to move on.

When you are ready to let go of something from the past, it can help to do something tangible that symbolizes the release of the memory. Some people, for example, take small stones to a pond or lake, and with each stone they state a memory they desire to leave behind, then throw the stone into the lake, symbolizing the release and end of that memory's grip on them.

Once, when speaking at a conference about forgiveness and letting go of the past, I had a brilliant idea. I invited everyone to write on a piece of paper an element of their past they were ready to release in order to move forward in their lives. I then had everyone come up and throw their written memory into a large metal trash can. When they had all returned to their seats, I thought it would be dramatic to light the papers on fire so everyone could see their memory go up in smoke.

I was right about it being dramatic and even memorable. The fire burned much more than I had anticipated and sent billows of smoke up to the ceiling of the room we were meeting in. Too late, I realized this exercise would probably have worked better if we were outside, perhaps around a campfire, where the smoke wouldn't have set off the fire alarms, triggered the sprinkler system, caused water to spray down into the room, and soaked all the participants. Now that is what I call memorable!

The Bible is quite clear about whether or not we should focus on the circumstances and hurts of our past: "Forget the former things; do not dwell on the past" (Isa. 43:18). Where should we be focusing our attention instead? "See, I am doing a new thing! Now it springs up; do you not perceive it?" (v. 19).

There must be a lot of us out there who chronically brood about the past so much that we miss out on the fresh opportunity, the new circumstance, or the healed relationship. Perhaps it's more comfortable to settle into what we know so well. New experiences are far from comfortable. *What will it be like? How will it affect me? What if I can't handle it?* What if? What if?

Of course, there are people like my friend Jake, who brims with new ideas, new adventures, and new challenges. Sometimes he wears me out with his enthusiasm. Unlike me, when he thinks about something new, it is exciting for him. For me, the new is mostly just stressful. Eventually I can adapt to the new and find my way forward, but by the time I get on board, there is another new, so I'm still lagging behind everyone else.

The final message at the very end of the Bible reminds us, "He who was seated on the throne said, 'I am making everything new!'" (Rev. 21:5). We know this, and if we for the most part believe it, then why is it still difficult for us to let go of the baggage from the past and embrace the challenges and opportunities of today?

I clipped out an old Peanuts cartoon in which Charlie Brown is standing on the pitching mound and Lucy walks up and tosses the ball to him. "Sorry I missed that easy fly ball," she says. "I thought I had it, but suddenly I remembered all the others I've missed . . . the past got in my eyes!"

Pressing On

Trying to not think of something is probably the most effective way to make sure it's all you think about. *Fuhgeddaboudit* is much more than trying to not think about the past. It is an invitation for us to start moving forward with freedom and confidence. Here are some steps than can help us turn from our past toward a positive future.

1. *Take time to learn from the past without staying stuck in it.* Ignoring or denying the past will not result in freedom. We can reflect on some of our negative experiences and painful memories from a brand-new perspective. Ask yourself what really happened. This time, though, approach it like the detective in *Dragnet*: "Just the facts, ma'am." Don't bother with blaming or trying

to figure out the whys and wherefores. When you have made note of the facts, then consider the emotions you feel about the situation.

After you've considered your feelings, it's time to think about how you can use this to help you be stronger and better today. Then it's time to move on. It's good to consider the things of the past, as long as we don't dwell on them. After doing this exercise, resist the temptation to gather up all the hurts and memories to tuck away for future wallowing. It's time to fuhgeddaboudit.

2. *Think about who you want to be now.* We are not trapped, and the things we endured or experienced don't have to define us. Just because we were victimized doesn't mean we have to be a victim now. Just because we failed doesn't make us a failure now. Just because our hearts are broken doesn't mean we won't love or be loved again. It may seem normal to hold on to past pain, but it is also normal to let it go when we are ready.

3. *Burn that bridge when you get to it.* Sometimes there are people, places, and things that constantly remind us of past hurts. It's possible to cut them off. Disconnect from anything you associate with the memory. Let go of the things that you connect with the pain. Avoid the triggers and reminders that keep pulling you back into the pain. Jesus dealt with this by releasing his followers: "If anyone will not welcome you or listen to your words, leave that home or town and shake the dust off your feet" (Matt. 10:14). Sometimes the right thing to do is physically get away. Perhaps it's a gift to walk away from the rejection and move on with your life. Trust your instinct;

you will know who is good for you and who isn't. Imagine starting over surrounded by people who encourage and support you, not those who are toxic and abusive.

4. *Forgive yourself and others.* Forgiveness helps release the anger and pain that haunt the past. When we forgive others, it helps us far more than them. We can assume they'll never own up to the damage they did, but it doesn't matter. As soon as we choose to release them and forgive, a tremendous weight falls away from us. It's not easy but it is essential.

5. *Start again—with gratitude.* Don't think this transformation is easy or painless, because it's not. I love the part of C. S. Lewis's *The Voyage of the Dawn Treader* in which Aslan, the lion, peels away the dragon skin from Eustace:

> The very first tear he made was so deep that I thought it had gone right into my heart. And when he began pulling the skin off, it hurt worse than anything I've ever felt. The only thing that made me able to bear it was just the pleasure of feeling the stuff peel off. . . .
>
> And there was I as smooth and soft as a peeled switch and smaller than I had been. Then he caught hold of me—I didn't like that much for I was very tender underneath now that I'd no skin on—and threw me into the water. It smarted like anything but only for a moment. After that it became perfectly delicious and as soon as I started swimming and splashing I found that all the pain had gone from my arm. And then I saw why. I'd turned into a boy again.[2]

"If anyone is in Christ," Paul writes, "he is a new creation. The old has passed away; behold, the new has come" (2 Cor.

29

5:17 ESV). Knowing that the old has passed away and the new has come helps us realize we are all living in the present right this second. We can't live in the past, and we certainly can't live in the future.

Sometimes I think I dwell on past successes and failures because I'm afraid the present won't be very good. This can feel safe because the past is all I know, which can make *now* seem a bit unsettling. Believe me, there are times I wish I could turn back the clock and do things differently, though the chances of that happening are pretty small. So I need to accept the gift of forgiveness and accept the fact that I need to be forgiven in the first place.

I also need to look around and take an honest assessment of here and now, which includes learning how to be present in today's issues, conversations, struggles, and celebrations. No more hanging back or sitting on the sidelines where I may feel safe and protected. No more thinking about how I used to be somebody and now I'm somebody else. I know things will be different than they were, and that is okay with me. My life is different than it was and different than it will be, but the Lord promised to never leave me, so it's time to stop lagging behind and step forward with gratitude. It's time to fuhgeddaboudit; after all, there's no future in the past.

3

It's All about Freedom

Learn from yesterday, live for today, hope for tomorrow. — Albert Einstein

Who doesn't want to be free? I hate to feel restricted or held back in any way. It's no secret that most of us have a deep longing to live without being held back by bonds, expectations, or irrational rules. Throughout my life, I've gravitated toward heroes who fought against anything that held them back. In movies, books, and music, I've been drawn to the antiheroes who remind me that freedom is worth fighting for and worth living for.

Sometimes we forget that God also cares about our freedom. Christ came in order that we could be free. Paul writes, "For freedom Christ has set us free" (Gal. 5:1 ESV). Yet for the most part we don't live our lives experiencing the freedom God intended when he first thought of us. Too often we feel trapped, held back, unable to soar or attain the freedom and joy that seem to elude us on a regular basis.

In the Sunday morning comics section, Garfield the cat, dressed a little like Rambo, breaks into a pet store as a freedom fighter. He runs through the pet store throwing open the cages of all the animals. "You're free, you're free!" he howls. All the cats, dogs, and birds just stay in their cages and look at him. Garfield says, "I guess folks must not be into freedom too much these days." Then he runs through the pet store slamming all the cages shut, saying, "You're secure, you're secure!"

There is something about freedom that attracts us and at the same time scares us a little. Maybe this is why we don't leap into our newfound freedom when offered it. Rather, we choose to hold back and, in the process, miss the great freedom God has in mind for each of us.

Freedom From and Freedom For

Maybe we aren't sure what freedom means for us. I see freedom as having two parts: freedom *from* and freedom *for*. In the Bible we see this demonstrated in the freedom from anything that takes us away from God. This includes anything that distances us from our true humanity and takes us away from being the holy, lovable people he made us to be. On the other hand, we have freedom for living a full, meaningful, abundant life. We are free to grow and move forward in a purposeful life.

"In order to be healthy," writes Frederick Buechner,

> there are certain rules you can break only at your peril. . . .
> Avoid bottles marked poison, don't jump out of boats unless
> you can swim, etc. In order to be happy, there are also certain
> rules you can break only at your peril . . . get rid of hatred and
> envy, tell the truth, avoid temptations to evil you're not strong

enough to resist, don't murder, steal, etc. . . . Both sets of rules
. . . describe not the way people feel life ought to be but the way
they have found it is.[1]

Perhaps that's just the way life is. But we don't have to lower
ourselves to accommodate a dying world. Rather, we have freedom and the power to break the mold and overcome the very
things that could enslave us. Paul reminds us we are free from
having to live in the futility, stupidity, and darkened understanding of those who don't know God. Then he goes on to say
we have freedom from the "old self, which is being corrupted
by its deceitful desires" (Eph. 4:22). We also have freedom for
putting on the new self, created to be like God, with true righ-
teousness and holiness.

We have freedom from being controlled by others, from
negative restraints, from having our decisions limited or our
choices made by others. We are also free from being held back
by debilitating habits or behaviors such as addiction, lying,
stealing, laziness, bitterness, and so on.

The other half of freedom, what can be considered positive
freedom, means that we have freedom for making our own decisions and choices without interference or limitations from others.
We also have freedom to choose how we relate to people by dem-
onstrating kindness, compassion, and forgiveness both for ourselves and for others. In Romans 6, we see that we have freedom
from the bondage of sin, as "we are those who have died to sin"
(v. 2), and freedom for being "alive to God in Christ Jesus" (v. 11).

These two sides of freedom were very important during the
time of our nation's founding. Our country established freedom from taxation without representation, cruel and unusual
punishment, limiting our expression of opinion, or being held

back from voting as we choose. Even as these negative freedoms were guaranteed, positive freedoms were also significantly included, such as the freedom to bear arms and the freedom to life, liberty, and the pursuit of happiness.

We are always letting go with one hand while taking hold with the other. This is the dynamic nature of freedom. We are in the process of being pulled out of that which binds us and taking hold of that which gives our lives meaning, purpose, and significance. This is the freedom to which we have been called.

True Freedom

Sometimes we get the idea that we want the thrill of total unrestrained freedom. Gordon MacKenzie, former creativity director for Hallmark cards, describes what might happen when we pursue total freedom.

What if I had a passion for unbridled freedom and high excitement of living fully? . . . That's it, I'll take up sky diving. I make the call, I sign up for the training required to jump out of an airplane. . . .

I am amazed at the ease with which the others tumble out into the cloudless sky. Now it is my turn. . . .

My mind screams, "You wanted more freedom, more excitement in your life. Well, you sure got it big-time!" The rush is incredible. I have a breath-taking sense of being alive—not sure for how long, but a tremendous sense of being alive. Miraculously, my parachute opens and I drift gracefully down to a safe landing. What a buzz! . . . Every Sunday for the next six months I'm back for another excitement hit.

It is now the first weekend of the seventh month. Here I am, making my third jump of the day. . . . As the landscape zooms up towards me, I find myself thinking, "I wonder what's for dinner?" . . .

Where did the life expanding thrill of my first jump go? Nothing lasts. I refuse to accept the loss. I have got to recreate the mind-blowing intoxication of my earlier jumps, but how? A little voice inside me whispers, "Unbuckle your parachute." I'm so impatient to get the old excitement back, I seize upon this idea without really thinking it through. . . . The excitement potion skyrockets. Every molecule in my body is screaming, "FREEE!" Splat. . . . I don't live to share the experience with anyone. So, skydiving without a parachute equals suicide. Total freedom is suicide.[2]

Freedom is important. But don't use it in such a way that you end up destroying the very freedom you want and God wants for you.

We have clashes inside us. Things just don't seem right. What we want to do is a struggle because we know it's not what we are supposed to be doing. Sometimes the things we are doing guarantee we'll never get what we're longing for.

There is a tension at work here, a tension between wanting our own way and wanting to live and be healthy. We want to be in loving relationships, but we want them to be the way we want them to be.

After more than four decades of marriage, my wife, Eileen, still hasn't become the person I wanted her to change into. And she will tell you that she still has not been able to fix me or help me become the person she thought I should be. You may want things your way, and to always be right, but then when you say you want to be in loving relationships, well, guess what: you can't have both.

Swiss physician Paul Tournier writes,

Our human condition can never escape from the tension between irreconcilable aspirations. We can't give way to both of them at once. We can only give free play first to one then the other at the right time. A musician cannot play a "doe" without first silencing the "ray" and all the other notes. They can't play the other notes without silencing the "doe," or plan on not producing anything harmonious but a frightful cacophony. Making music means playing notes at the right time. We can never satisfy our moral impulses all at the same time.

There is no life without repression. We cannot be generous without repressing our egotism. Or give way to egotism without repressing our generosity. We can't give free rein to our fancy except by repressing our need for order. Or give way to our need for order, without clipping the wings of our fancy.

In the adult there is no laughter that does not hide secret tears. Nor are there any tears behind which there isn't some repressed enjoyment. There is no giving without some reticence, and there's no withholding without some longing to give.[3]

God wants us to know true freedom, where we become the unique, unrepeatable miracle he made us to be. Yet sometimes we realize it's not working out the way we had hoped. It's because we can't have our way all the time, in every situation, and experience life as it was meant to be. We don't get to have it both ways. It's only when we allow God to take over our lives and we submit our will to him that we begin to experience real freedom.

I remember getting to the place where I was unhappy with living my life solely on my terms, with my limited resources, all the while feeling bound up and definitely not very free. So, when I asked Christ to come into my life, I reminded him that I needed some real help. I told him I had a bunch of personal garbage I'd accumulated along the way, and I asked for a whole bunch of forgiveness. Then I confessed I was bound up in a lot of ways, and I needed his freedom.

The response I got was something like, *Do you know how long I've been waiting for you to ask for my help? I've been waiting years for you to finally stop trying to make it on your own. And I'm happy to come in and give you freedom and forgiveness, a fresh start, the power to go forward, and wisdom in difficult situations. I'll actually love through you, if you find it difficult to love some people. Just let me be Lord of your life, and you can be truly free.* Well, that was an offer I couldn't refuse.

Of course, I could have refused. "God's terrible insistence on human freedom is so absolute that he granted us the power to live as though He did not exist, to spit in His face, to crucify Him."[4]

With freedom we have lots of choices; some are minor and fairly insignificant, and some are huge and meaningful. When Moses, their leader, was about to die, the Hebrews were given a monumental choice. God said in so many words, "Today I put before you a choice: life and death!" Then he gave them a hint, "Choose life" (see Deut. 30:18–19). I can imagine some of the people thinking, *What kind of choice is that?* But it was still their decision to make. In the same way, we have the freedom to choose. Day by day, minute by minute, situation by situation, we can choose life. Then we discover that what God wants for us is what we've wanted all along. He gives us freedom as a gift.

If we are going to experience true freedom, we need to understand a little about what it is. There are many definitions, although one of my favorites, to paraphrase Kris Kristofferson, is that freedom is another way of saying we are at the point of not having anything else to lose. Perhaps he was reminding us that as long as we cling to our baggage, holding on with all our strength, we are never really free. It's only when we choose to let go that we start to know freedom.

Too Many Choices

I used to think the way to experience greater freedom was to have more and more choices. It made sense to me because I thought that if my choices became too limited, I might feel inhibited or imprisoned, which is not freedom at all.

I have many friends who struggle when it comes to committing in a relationship. They may love their significant other and may even want to get married. Then uneasiness starts to creep into their minds; soon they start worrying about how they might lose their freedom if they commit to one person "until death do us part." The very thought of marriage scares them because it appears on the surface to take away their sense of freedom. That is a great misunderstanding.

Having an infinite number of choices doesn't actually result in greater freedom. This principle is true whether we consider a big issue like whom we will marry or something slightly smaller, like what kind of jam we will put on our toast. According to a study at Columbia University, when people were faced with smaller rather than larger varieties of jam, they were actually more satisfied with their tasting and even bought more jam.[5] The reality is that having too many choices results in paralysis instead of freedom.

There was a time I loved the idea of eating at The Cheesecake Factory. Talk about choices! Their menu is like a coffee-table book with bright colors, page after laminated page of dining options. It is literally an international bazaar of food selections from around the world. And they serve great food. Even now,

I marvel at how they are able to prepare and serve so many different kinds of meals seemingly without effort or stress. I'm impressed! Picking up the hefty menu, I'd skip the pages of appetizers and head straight to the dozens of burger options, which also include several different kinds of vegetarian burgers to choose from.

Then someone at the table inevitably would bring up the Italian options, which included many Mediterranean entrées thrown in just to allow for more choices. But what about the Mexican foods, and the Tex-Mex just for kicks? The pages of Asian foods include (not in any particular order) Chinese (Szechwan and Mandarin, of course), Korean, Japanese, Thai, and Vietnamese mixed in with some Indian dishes (from both the northern and southern cuisines).

Of course, closer to home we have good old American food, including West Coast fusion and Southern standards such as fried chicken right alongside some Cajun and Creole dishes such as jambalaya and the similar alternative of Spanish paella. There's Midwestern steaks and New England chowders and even Pacific Northwest specialties such as salmon (silver, Coho, and king). The salad options all look good, and I'm not even going to go into the pages of specialty drinks to complement the meal. Coke or Pepsi? Forget that—there seem to be infinite combinations to quench your thirst. Finally we get to the namesake dessert option: cheesecake. How many different kinds of cheesecake are there? You'll find out when you visit The Cheesecake Factory.

By the time we are ready to order, I'm exhausted. I'm also confused and overwhelmed, and a little bit afraid because I don't want to make a mistake and choose the wrong thing. When the waitperson looks to me, I freeze. *Oh no, what am I going to do? What if I pick something then find out I should have picked something else instead?*

In that moment of crisis and indecision, I get a brilliant idea. "What do you suggest?" I ask. While the people at my table groan, the waitperson describes a couple of choices that they happen to like. Then, looking down in shame, I mumble to the server to bring whatever it was they happened to suggest in that moment. Too many choices does not result in freedom, it results in paralysis!

In his book *Paradox of Choice*, psychologist Barry Schwartz explains why too many choices can make people miserable.

> When people have no choice, life is almost unbearable. As the number of available choices increases, as it has in our consumer culture, the autonomy, control, and liberation this variety brings are powerful and positive. But as the number of choices keeps growing, negative aspects of having a multitude of options begin to appear. As the number of choices grows further, the negatives escalate until we become overloaded. At this point, choice no longer liberates, but debilitates. It might even be said to tyrannize.[6]

Evidently, both extremes are bad for us. Too few choices and too many choices make our lives more difficult and take away our freedom and the joy it brings. What emotional churning below the surface is causing us to freeze up when there are too many choices?

The first emotional roadblock we come to is *regret*, or even anticipated regret. What if we choose wrong? Or what if we don't like what we ordered? Sometimes just considering that we might feel regret, or the anticipation that regret is coming, makes choosing very difficult. Sometimes even thinking we might regret our choice can block us from freely and joyfully choosing, even when the choice is as meaningless as which flavor of cheesecake we want to eat.

A second blockage we must face is *opportunity cost*. This business-sounding phrase refers to missing out or giving up something every time one alternative is chosen over another. Imagine my potential dismay at The Cheesecake Factory if I order the peanut butter cheesecake then realize I could have had the Oreo or Snickers cheesecake like someone ordered at the next table. Every choice has a cost. The car you want to buy costs money that you will no longer have to spend on a summer vacation.

These decisions we make as we go through a typical day are often small and fairly insignificant, unlike the big, momentous decisions that can drive us crazy. Choosing between vanilla or strawberry ice cream is a small enough decision that we don't worry about it because we are only choosing between two fairly equal treats.

But as a kid, when I visited Baskin-Robbins with my family, there were thirty-one flavors! Now opportunity costs were suddenly a big obstacle. I would pace up and down along their counter, trying to decide what flavor to order, realizing that once I made my very important decision, there would be thirty flavors I would not be able to eat. Is it any wonder that the number one most frequently ordered flavor at Baskin-Robbins's thirty-one-flavor shops is (wait for it) vanilla?

The third obstacle to choosing, when there are many available choices, is that our *expectations* keep growing. When we have low expectations, it's easy to be thrilled with whichever way our experience turns out. But as our expectations grow, we tend to become less and less satisfied with certain outcomes. Since there is a tendency for us to pin our hopes for happiness on fulfilled expectations, we are also setting ourselves up for disappointment when these greater expectations go unmet.

Of course, there is nothing wrong with this way of thinking if our expectations are grounded in experiences that give us good reason to have them. However, if I believe that my expectations alone will bring me what I want, I'm using something called "magical thinking" and setting myself up for even greater disappointment.

When children are little, they have a difficult time understanding that thinking something doesn't make it true. According to developmental psychologist Jean Piaget, children sometimes believe that their thoughts can directly cause things to happen.[7] For example, thinking angry thoughts about your little brother can cause him to fall down the stairs.

Imagine a child confiding to a friend that he or she doesn't like Aunt Sally, only to hear the next day that Aunt Sally was in a car accident and was taken to the hospital. The assumption that their thoughts and feelings were so powerful as to cause such tragedy has the potential to traumatize the child. Piaget called this "magical thinking" and suggested we all grow out of it at around seven years of age.

If only he were right! How many grown-ups still practice some form of magical thinking in their lives? We think something is going to happen in a particular way, so we expect it. Then when it doesn't happen we are disappointed, frustrated, and resentful of the one who let us down.

Choosing Our Expectations

For thirteen years, my wife, Eileen, and I had a dog named Maggie. She was a King Charles Cavalier that, in spite of being quite cute, had a terrible personality disorder. After we'd spent hundreds of dollars for basic dog training, the professional trainer surrendered and told us to stop wasting money; Maggie was completely untrainable. If that wasn't bad enough, she liked Eileen but let it be known she didn't particularly like me. Whenever I'd walk into a room where she was, she would give me a look very similar to those I'd received from some of the girls I'd dated in high school. The look combined disappointment with haughtiness, as if to say, "Oh, it's you. . . . It would be so nice if you weren't here."

In time, Maggie trained me to have extremely low expectations for our relationship. Because of her excellent training of me, I didn't expect her to respond in a positive way toward me, and I was rarely disappointed.

Eventually, she went to doggie heaven (I'm being generous here, because the Bible doesn't mention doggie purgatory). We then welcomed a new puppy, another King Charles Cavalier, named Gabbie. What a difference! Gabbie loves me. She wants me to be with her, go on walks, and feed her snacks, all of which I'm more than happy to do because she is so responsive. Whenever I drive up to the house, Gabbie knows the sound of my car, so she runs to the window, jumping with excitement and joy at the mere thought that I am about to walk in the door.

Based on my experience with Gabbie, I expect her to be zealous in her devotion to me, and I even feel like maybe I have a special charm with dogs. My expectation is natural and appropriate. Imagine the crushing disappointment I would feel if I walked into the room and Gabbie responded like the indifferent Maggie and gave me "that look." I'd be devastated because my expectations are now very high. However, if I'd ever expected a warm, caring welcome from Maggie, that would be an example of magical thinking. I would've been setting myself up for disappointment and resentment. Perhaps the same was true with my high school girlfriends.

When we choose positive freedom (freedom *for*), we can remain free at our inner core, even if our negative freedom is taken away by others. This means we can have a deep well of personal positive freedom no matter how our external conditions change.

Viktor Frankl witnessed the power of positive freedom while living among his fellow prisoners in a Nazi concentration camp, Theresienstadt. Though every shred of external freedom was taken from them by the Nazi guards, he describes the glimmer of inner freedom that existed beneath the surface of some of his fellow prisoners.

> In spite of all the enforced physical and mental primitiveness of the life in the concentration camp, it was possible for spiritual life to deepen. Sensitive people who were used to a rich intellectual life may have suffered much pain . . . but the damage to their inner selves was less. They were able to retreat from their terrible surroundings to a life of inner riches and spiritual freedom. Only in this way can one explain the apparent paradox that some prisoners of a less hardy makeup often seemed to survive camp life better than did those of a robust nature. . . .
>
> The experiences of camp life show that man does have a choice of action. There were enough examples, often of a heroic nature, which proved that apathy could be overcome, irritability suppressed. Man can preserve a vestige of spiritual freedom, of independence of mind, even in such terrible conditions of psychic and physical stress.
>
> We who lived in concentration camps can remember the men who walked through the huts comforting others, giving away

their last piece of bread. They may have been few in number, but they offer sufficient proof that everything can be taken from a man but one thing: the last of human freedoms—to choose one's attitude in any given set of circumstances, to choose one's own way.[8]

My uncle Fred Kuraner was also a survivor of a Nazi concentration camp. Although he survived, he lost his father, mother, and brother, as well as his young bride, all murdered by the Nazis. The few times I heard him recall some of his painful experiences, he also chose to cling to a deep inner conviction that life mattered and he was free to love and be loved. In spite of everything, he chose life, and he was a free man.

The Power of (Positive/Negative) Thinking

To love is to suffer. To avoid suffering one must not love. But then one suffers from not loving. Therefore, to love is to suffer; not to love is to suffer; to suffer is to suffer. To be happy, then, is to suffer, but suffering makes one unhappy. Therefore, to be happy one must love or love to suffer or suffer from too much happiness. — Woody Allen

Being a negative thinker is not so bad. In fact, for me it seems to come quite naturally. I've spent a long time perfecting the skills required to become an accomplished negative thinker, not that they are giving awards to people with dysfunctional habits. Perhaps my negativity goes hand in hand with my experience as a lifelong depressor. I can't recall very many times in my life when I wasn't depressed to some degree, or negative in my thinking.

For the most part, I didn't see this as a problem to be solved; it was just the way I was inside and the way I related to the world outside. In the novel *The World According to Garp*, the "Under Toad" was a larger-than-life creature Garp's young son, Walt, imagined sucking him down under the water ever since he had been warned to "Watch out for the undertow."[1] I think I took that warning to heart, and spent many years on watch for the undertow that would pull me down. Every beautiful day at the beach was an opportunity to be pulled out to sea by unseen forces and every walk in the park was a chance to step in dog droppings. You get the point.

Surprisingly, these negative traits didn't seem to hold me back. Perhaps I learned to use them in ways that made me a better friend, coworker, counselor, speaker, and writer. I think people got used to my eccentric ways of looking at life, perhaps thinking, *Oh, that's just the way he is.*

Once, while serving on the board of a mission organization with Robert Schuller, I received a "Possibility Thinker's Calendar" from the Crystal Cathedral. Every month there were beautiful pictures of people doing incredible things. When I showed it to our staff, they seemed confused as to why I would even have such a positive thing.

It wasn't very long after that staff meeting when I received a gift from my colleagues. Opening it, I found they had created an "Impossibility Thinker's Calendar" for me. Each month featured a picture of a staff person in a terrible situation, being overwhelmed and crushed beneath the burden of whatever they were attempting. One picture even featured our youth pastor on the roof of the church preparing to jump off, despairing of working with high school kids. I guess they understood, after all, how my mind worked.

Recognize Your Filter

For many years, my friend Randy Rowland and I cohosted the radio show *Everyday People* on the NBC affiliate station in Seattle. One of my favorite interviews on our program was the time we sat down with legendary author Norman Vincent Peale and his wife, Ruth. Randy and I met them at a conference and were surprised when they agreed to be interviewed on the show. Norman was best known for his book *The Power of Positive Thinking* and renowned for his insights on and encouragement of people living intentionally positive lives.

Randy was a little worried how someone as obviously negative as I was would be able to sit in the same room, much less conduct an interview, with such an icon of positive thinking. I was wondering the same thing.

When the interview started, I wanted to include Ruth right away, so I turned to her and asked, half jokingly, "Isn't it true that even though he wrote the book *The Power of Positive Thinking*, Norman is really a very negative person?"

I almost fell off my chair when she responded, "Oh, that is so true! He always thinks the worst about things and gets discouraged when he sees problems all around us. I told him, 'Norman, write this book because it will help you with your problems!'"

I wasn't expecting that response. Turning to Norman, I asked if this was true. "Oh, yes," he said. "I've struggled with negative thoughts, and I'd easily get discouraged and want to give up when problems seemed to pile up around me." Then he added, "But I discovered, with Jesus in my life, I could live beyond myself! So, every day I choose to be positive and allow the Lord to work through me."

Thinking back on that encounter, I'm struck with Norman's and Ruth's honesty. And I'm impressed that they recognized and frankly talked about life realistically. But what impacted me most was Norman's realization that with Jesus he could live beyond himself. I wanted Jesus to help me live beyond myself too.

We all have limitations, blind spots, and weaknesses that can hold us back. But those limitations don't have to be the final word on our worth or usefulness in life. Perhaps, like he did for Norman Vincent Peale, God makes it possible for us to live way beyond our limited resources, cleverness, and natural ability.

Since that day back in 1987, I've wanted to learn how we can live our lives fully and abundantly, regardless of our background or mental attitude. Everyone has a unique way of looking at the world. These mental filters are what turn our viewpoint toward positive or negative thinking. If we are to experience freedom and live like there is no yesterday, it is important to understand how our thinking can become distorted by the filters we use.

Using a mental filter is one way we distort our thinking. When someone uses a negative mental filter, they tend to pick out one adverse detail of their life or situation and obsess over it. This mulling or brooding over the negative aspect filters out any of the positive things that have also occurred. It can start to feel as though only negative things happen to us all the time. By losing sight of the positive elements of our lives, we even stop noticing them, and it's as if they never occurred.

If we find ourselves filtering, it is important to counter this tendency by putting even more focus on positive things. Make a list of each positive thing that occurs, no matter how small or insignificant it may seem. We actually have many more positive things in a typical day than we ever remember. Writing down each conversation, kindness, achievement, and appreciation allows us to counter the influence of negative filtering. It may seem strange and even difficult at first to come up with any, but as we do it, it becomes easier to recognize and feel good about the positives in our lives.

Filtering is found frequently in people who struggle with depression or an anxiety disorder. Negative filtering increases our tendency toward feelings of depression, loneliness, and worthlessness. Anxiety tends to rise when positive aspects of our circumstances are filtered out while the self-defeating thoughts are magnified.

The Myths of Positive Thinking

There is a lot of misunderstanding about what is meant by positive thinking. We see it mentioned in slogans, self-help books, "name it and claim it" churches, motivational workshops, and advertising. Phrases like "Just do it!" "You can achieve what your mind can conceive!" "Think and grow rich!" and "Turn your scars into stars!" are everywhere. The popularity of this approach creates a momentum that leads people to assume ideas that aren't actually true.

Myth #1: Positive Thinking Is Easy

I know it seems simple, and listening to some people talk about the benefits of thinking positively makes it seem like a no-brainer. Apparently all we have to do is flip a switch in our brain and our negative perspectives will all change to shiny bright positive things that, in turn, will make life great. The reality is much more strenuous. It's a process of learning new ways to think and respond to life situations. We have to retrain our brains to think in intentionally different ways. This takes time, effort, and a commitment to switch how we think.

Myth #2: Positive Thinking Means You Are Happy All the Time

This may be the biggest misunderstanding of positive thinking. It isn't like *The Stepford Wives*, where everyone smiles and robotically responds with clichés and affirmations. Of course, positive thinkers have times of sadness and defeat. It wouldn't be human to never be sad. God has given us a whole range of emotions to respond to life in a complicated, chaotic, and difficult world. Rather than hide our feelings, we can, in every situation, be grateful and focus on the blessings we have rather than on everything we lack.

Myth #3: Positive Thinking Protects You from Bad Things Happening

This myth is dangerous because it sets people up for disappointment and ultimately despair. Regardless of the popularity of songs like, "Don't Worry, Be Happy," life is more than dancing around and filling our heads with nonsensical thoughts like *Every little thing will be all right.* The truth is that everything will not always be all right. Having a positive mindset can help you remain rooted and optimistic in hard times, but it won't stop the hard times from coming. Heartbreak is a fact of life, and we will all live to see people we love pass away. Another reality of life in this world is the presence of sin. People will do you wrong, cheat you, hurt you, and lie to you. We can still choose to live in hope for a brighter future. Even the worst circumstances can have good found in them; depending on our perspective, we can embrace the good.

Myth #4: Positive Thinking Means You Won't Have Negative Thoughts

We don't just will ourselves to never have negative thoughts. We will have whatever thoughts we have. Some people mistakenly think that all they need to do is replace a negative thought with a more positive one. But that isn't the answer. This issue brings up the important point that regardless of what thoughts come into our minds, we can choose which ones we will focus on. Sitting and brooding about some negative idea won't help, but we can choose to engage with the positive thoughts and give our attention to them.

Negative thoughts are natural and part of our mental functioning and shouldn't be hindered. Rather, they can be replaced with ideas that are more accurate and useful. While this doesn't do away with negative thoughts, it does help a person consider other sides of their situation without allowing the negative elements to grab hold and dominate their thoughts or actions.

Myth #5: Positive Thinking Is a Cure-All That Forever Changes Your Life for the Good

There is no universal remedy that changes our lives forever so that only good things happen and everything is easy. Positive thinking is not a magic bullet that instantly fixes everything and resolves all our issues. It does provide help and gives a supportive boost so we can rise above a negative experience, reframe it, look at it from another perspective, and find new and creative solutions we hadn't considered before.

Not surprisingly, there has been far more emphasis on issues related to the negative aspects of our thinking and acting. The vast majority of therapists, psychologists, and medical practitioners focus almost exclusively on negatives in our lives. Abraham Maslow, as long ago as 1954, said,

> The science of psychology has been far more successful on the negative than on the positive side. It has revealed to us much about man's shortcomings, his illness, his sins, but little about his potentialities, his virtues, his achievable aspirations, or his full psychological height. It is as if psychology has voluntarily restricted itself to only half its rightful jurisdiction, and that, the darker, meaner half.[2]

Being negative is not always bad. We can use it to better our lives, and it can also serve the purpose of helping us grow in positive ways. It isn't negative to ask good questions, especially when they lead to improving situations. Whether positive or negative, we need to be real. Sometimes how we express ourselves can make all the difference.

Being positive is not always good, particularly if we hide behind positivity and pretend nothing needs to change. For example, national cancer researchers found that people who played down their risk of heart disease were more likely to show early signs of it.[3]

Being super positive is not better than being super negative. To have an authentic life, we need both sides. Being constantly positive doesn't guarantee a happy, meaningful life; being *real* does.

Merely thinking positively doesn't actually move us forward in our lives. We also need to acknowledge obstacles and hindrances that must be overcome. This grounding is beneficial because it moves us toward action. We start the transition from being dreamers to doers. This opens the door to explore the power of negative thinking.

The Negative Path to Happiness

It seems counterintuitive to think we might be happier with a negative mindset, though it is surprising to visit developing countries and discover a level of satisfaction and happiness that often is much greater than among those in more financially secure countries.

Ancient Stoics of Greece and Rome determined that the best way to handle an uncertain future was not to focus on the best scenario but rather to focus on the worst possibilities. Evidently, seriously thinking about worst-case scenarios, what the Stoics called "the premeditation of evils,"[4] actually diminishes their power to hurt or hold us back. Applying this strategy from ancient times is considered "defensive pessimism." Positive thinking involves trying to convince ourselves that everything will work out fine, which subtly reinforces the belief that it would be horrible if things didn't turn out the way we hoped.

By setting low expectations and envisioning worst-case scenarios, studies have shown, defensive pessimists actually optimized their performance on a variety of tasks, from darts and math problems to fulfilling real-life goals. This also applies to long-term lifetime satisfaction. Older adults who had underestimated their future satisfaction were less likely than their optimistic peers to end up disabled or die prematurely.

The significant value that comes from negative thinking won't be having more upbeat feelings or even experiencing more success. Its value is simply sheer realism. We can embrace the uncertainty of life and recognize that things can go terribly wrong as well as (unexpectedly) right. This even applies to the big negative that is often most difficult to deal with: our own death. It is a fact of life that no one escapes. Woody Allen summed up many people's attitudes toward death when he quipped, "I'm strongly against it."[5] Whether we are positive thinkers or negative thinkers, death is a reality we aren't going to avoid or wish away.

Positive thinking can backfire on us because it can trick us into thinking everything will turn out well, so we can relax, thus making it harder for us to get our work done or our goals met.

> Decades of research have found that positive thinking isn't always so positive. In some cases, pessimists fare better than those with a sunnier disposition. Married couples who were extremely optimistic about their relationship's future were more likely to experience relationship deterioration. Optimism may also be tied to lower earnings. A study of data from British households found that across two decades, especially optimistic self-employed people earned about 25 percent less than their pessimistic peers.[6]

Surprisingly, it is negative thinkers who are the best innovators when it comes to getting things done. Negative thinkers are tuned in to the challenges to be faced. Identifying potential obstacles and discovering strategies to overcome them is an automatic response for negative thinkers facing difficulties. They also are thinking of solutions before others are even aware there may be a problem.

Negative thinkers aren't pessimists like people assume; they are merely committed realists. They are invaluable on planning teams because they see not only problems but also opportunities that others might miss or ignore.

Regardless of where you may fall on the positive/negative scale, there is much we can learn from the way others think, and our lives can improve greatly if, like Norman Vincent Peale, we discover that with Jesus in our lives, we can live beyond ourselves.

5

Binocular Vision— Seeing with 20/20 Distortion

If I paint a wild horse, you might not see the horse... but surely you will see the wildness! — Pablo Picasso

When I was young I thought binoculars were magical—just the idea that I could hold them up to my eyes and see distant objects and people up close. But the day I discovered the other end was over the top! Turning the binoculars around and looking at things that were nearby and seeing them become smaller and seemingly far away was kind of like *Honey, I Shrunk the Kids*.

Of course, all technology we don't understand seems like magic to us. But I was still excited. Little did I know that the same binocular effect takes place in our minds without our even being aware of it. We have a tendency to distort experiences and perceptions by enlarging some things in our minds while diminishing others. One of the most common distortions is to magnify negative events and minimize positive things. Which end of the binoculars we choose to look through will have great impact on our perceptions, attitudes, and behaviors.

This is one of many mental distortions that occur frequently in life. We may assume that what we see is clear and accurate, but in reality, we may be experiencing distortions in our thinking that need to be recognized, understood, and adjusted.

Binocular Vision

In relationships, "binocular vision" is often referred to as the ability to see and align another person's viewpoint alongside your own, and to see yourself through the other person's eyes. To relate with someone else, it isn't enough to only see things your way but rather to hold both views at the same time. "With binocular vision, you don't give up your perspective; you enrich it through a deeper understanding of your partner's perspective."[1]

Many relationships struggle because we easily see and express our own opinions, needs, and views without being able to recognize and understand the other person's perspective, wants, and viewpoints.

When we focus only on our own issues, without considering the other person's, it becomes difficult to grow together and solve problems with love and empathy. Perhaps there is no more lonely existence than being in a relationship with someone who only sees or cares about themselves.

This is illustrated well in the movie *Lost in Translation*. Bill Murray's character, struggling with old-guy angst, calls his wife back home in America, who seems to be only concerned with the color of carpet being installed in his office. Interrupting her, he shares, "Honey, I'm lost."

"What do you want me to do about it?" is her response.

He asks, "What would you like to do to help?"

"I've got to go," she answers, and hangs up the phone.[2]

Without empathy to help us relate in a meaningful way, we too often fall into a pattern of behavior that strives to get the other person to think, act, and feel the same way we do. Inevitably we end up feeling bad when others aren't like us or have different interests and tastes. This leads to communicating that something is wrong with them and they need to change to become more like us. Then, if they refuse to embrace our views, we are left feeling betrayed and resentful.

It is only when we are able to recognize their uniqueness while holding on to our own that we begin to navigate the challenges of growing relationships.

One of the difficulties is that sometimes our emotions feel differently on the inside than they appear on the outside. For example, when I am feeling hurt or resentful, others may see me as being mean or perhaps demanding. I don't intend to come across as a mean person, and from my point of view, my responses are justified because I think I'm being treated unfairly. This distortion of what we're feeling, or how we express it, can cause us to feel misunderstood, which in turn leads us to pull away, further isolating ourselves.

There is a sense of loneliness from feeling we are on the outside looking in, which in turn affects the ways we relate and communicate with others. "I'm an affectionate man," writes Douglas Coupland,

> but I have much trouble showing it. When I was younger, I used to worry so much about being alone, being unlovable or incapable of love. As the years went on, my worries changed. I worried that I would become incapable of having a relationship. I felt as though the world lived inside a warm house at night and I was outside. I couldn't be seen because I was out there in the night. Now I'm inside that house and it feels just the same. We can be surrounded with family, we can be surrounded with friends, we can be in loving relationships, we can be around people we hope will care for us and we still will feel lost. We will still feel alone and unlovable.[3]

Toddler Thinking

As we grow, our beliefs and opinions are reinforced by others who agree with us, which causes us to want to hang out with those who think like we do while avoiding those who think differently. Cliques and social groups take shape where we are exposed to mostly like-minded people. Our culture seemingly prides itself on creating giant, insurmountable dividing lines. These divisions are reinforced by rehashing messages we agree with while demeaning and belittling the "other side" for their crazy and ignorant views.

When we were little children, it didn't seem odd that we gravitated toward those who rewarded us with smiles, nods of affirmation, and overt praise. However, staying stuck in our infant mentality does not usually end well for our adult selves.

We've all known folks who get angry, defensive, and even aggressive when someone disagrees with them or holds a belief different from theirs. Their toddler thinking undermines their effectiveness at work, alienates others, and destroys those who could be loving, supportive people in their lives.

A friend asked me to meet for coffee because she was struggling to maintain a healthy relationship with her brother. Evidently, in a recent visit at her brother's home, he wanted to watch an old movie that was a favorite of his. She told him that she didn't want to see that movie again and suggested they might watch something else. That was all it took for a wellspring of anger and years of resentment to spew from her brother like a raging volcano.

As she prepared to leave, her brother approached her with an intense stare and asked the "big" question, which involved a particular elected official in our government. Without considering the ramifications, she told him what she thought, and that pushed him over the edge. Hurling abuse, shouting about how she was an ignoramus, he yelled at her that she was no longer his sister, nor was she part of his family. She was banned from ever setting foot in his home and was never to speak to him again for the rest of their lives!

No wonder she wanted to meet for coffee. I asked if this was the first time anything like this had occurred between them, and she told me about three or four other times she had been banished from his life.

When a young child throws a tantrum, hurls toys around the room, and screams about how much she hates her mother and perhaps her sister, we understand that the toddler is acting like a toddler—maybe one who needs a nap, but still it is toddler behavior and no one takes it too seriously. After all, most of us grow out of the "terrible twos."

But when a grown man is living and relating in his toddler brain, there can be serious ramifications. Childish thinking isn't all bad. In fact, it can be fun for a while. If we are to believe all the books, movies, and songs, we think that most of the time we fall in love or begin relationships with a toddler mindset, which is impulsive, emotional, and often volatile.

At first such a relationship seems to be filled with wonder and joy, but in time it usually crashes into conflict, pain, and frustration. Because young children are unable to experience binocular vision, the toddler mindset brings self-obsession with an inability to see another person's viewpoint. Adult love, in contrast, values compassion, empathy, and kindness, which are rooted in our ability to recognize and understand the other person's perspective.

"Most complaints in toddler love have this subtext: 'You need to be more like me. You need to think and feel like I do,'" says Steven Stosny. "Confusing intimacy with having their partners think and feel the same as they do, lovers in the toddler brain feel rejected and betrayed when their partners think and behave like the unique individuals they are."[4]

Black-and-White Thinking

According to the old joke, the world consists of two kinds of people: those who break everything down to "two kinds of people" and those who don't. Maybe it's just part of our human nature that we like to make sense of our world by dividing our perceptions into simple categories. We can easily become overwhelmed by the complexity of life around us and the sheer amount of information that bombards us daily.

Good or bad, friend or foe, angel or devil—we can reduce perceptions into simple categories and embrace or dismiss people and ideas quickly and easily. While there can be obvious benefits from this type of simplifying, there are also problems we need to address.

When a person engages in black-and-white thinking, they might see things as either/or, right or wrong, and all or nothing. Seeing only two sides of an issue may cause us to mistakenly ignore options that are reasonable and conducive to compromising and meeting in the middle. Unfortunately, many folks who see the world as black-and-white recoil from opportunities to compromise because they see it as losing or at least lowering their standards.

Tim Chaves, writing in *Forbes*, points out that black-and-white thinking in our professional lives can make us abandon projects due to mere bumps in the road because of feeling they are inevitably doomed to fail. Thus, when we encounter obstacles, instead of considering various options we think, *I should just quit because I'm no good* or *I should fire that person because she is difficult to work with.* The volatility of our changes dramatically affects the people with whom we work. Our all-or-nothing statements can create tension and unease in the workplace, making it difficult to work together and share new ideas and strategies.[5]

Like most people, I grew up with a tendency toward black-and-white thinking. It was easy to define others as being with me or against me, good or bad. Once I was telling a friend about another person whom I disliked and didn't trust. I blurted out, "He is just evil."

My friend paused and then said, "Maybe he is, but have you considered that he may just be very frightened, so he does hurtful things?"

I didn't want to consider other options. My mind was made up, and if I could dismiss someone as evil then I wouldn't have to deal with them anymore. But if there were more ways to approach this person—like perhaps he wasn't evil but rather afraid, insecure, lonely, or sad—then I'd probably need to stay in a relationship with him.

Life can be richer when we can see that people are not just smart or stupid, strong or weak, good or evil. We all have a mixture of strengths, hopes, fears, gifts, and negative traits inside us at the same time. Accepting our own and others' uniqueness can give a sense of freedom that is exhilarating.

While it's possible to move from black-and-white thinking to a healthier mindset, most of the time we don't recognize our own tendencies toward this type of thinking. Maybe because it is comfortable—and realistically, by now most people in our lives are there because we already think alike—it can be difficult to even realize when we've lumped people into narrow categories.

If we find ourselves using black-and-white thinking, much of the time we do it unintentionally, without thinking or even knowing it is happening. For this reason, it is helpful to pause and ask ourselves why we are viewing the situation in a certain way.

Families have communication habits that often teach a child how to think in simple categories. For example, my brother Karl was the "good" one. He was tall, handsome, confident, and popular. He surfed and played tennis, was class president of our high school, and effortlessly seemed to date the prettiest girls. On top of all this, he was a leader in church youth groups, always helpful and willing to lend a hand and teach others. What chance did I have?

I tended to be more troublesome. Now, don't get me wrong; I wanted to be good and popular and everything I admired in Karl, but somehow I had different experiences. I was in trouble more often than not. My mouth seemed to get me in hot water and kept me on the outside of most things. I was banned from Sunday school in fifth grade, and a few years later I was able to parlay that into being expelled from school for fighting. Although I intended to be a good Christian, the church folks thought I was more of a problem to be solved than someone to be included and affirmed.

It took decades for me to realize that Karl wasn't that good and I wasn't that bad. We were just different in some ways and alike in many other ways. We both had strengths and weaknesses, fears and hopes, abilities and shortcomings. Really, we were just two regular people who also happened to be brothers. Later in life we recognized that our experiences growing up were different, and our perceptions of what happened were quite different too, but we weren't good or bad. Just a lot of in-between.

Overgeneralizing

Overgeneralizing is a pattern of distortion that can lead to serious difficulties. When a person has an experience, then draws a faulty conclusion based on the one experience, they are overgeneralizing. Imagine you are driving to an appointment, maybe running a little late, and the traffic light turns red just as you get to the intersection. Sitting in the car, you mutter something like, "Why do I always get stuck at every red light?" Whenever we find ourselves saying *always*, *never*, and *every*, we are overgeneralizing.

"The drive-thru *always* gets my order wrong!" "*Every* time I go to the movies, someone sits right behind me and talks through the *whole* film." That last was a double overgeneralization, because the complaint combined *every* with *whole*. Surely there might have been parts of the film when the annoying person didn't talk.

There may be a close connection between overgeneralizing and feeling angry.

This tendency of overgeneralizing makes us angrier than when we use more realistic and accurate language. People who overgeneralize tend to get angrier than others, they express that anger in less healthy ways, and they suffer greater consequences as a result of their anger.[6]

Stereotyping people based on their race, age, political preferences—or really anything—is a damaging form of overgeneralizing. It's easier to write off whole groups of people than to actually treat people as distinct individuals.

I asked a friend recently why he wouldn't return my calls when I phoned him. He paused, took a deep breath, and shared with me that when he was a young teenager, his girlfriend broke his heart when she broke up with him during a phone call. He overgeneralized and concluded that girls would always break up with him on the phone, so he avoided talking on the phone with women he liked.

After a while, he realized that late night calls of any kind were always bad news, and a couple of times when he applied for jobs he was turned down with a phone call. He reasoned that phone calls always bring bad news, rejection, and end in a disaster, so he avoided talking to anyone on the phone when at all possible.

Fortunately, he had staff at work who could answer phones and return calls for him. At home, his wife checked messages and returned the calls. In this way he concealed his phone phobia and the distorted thinking that brought it about.

Listening to his story, I marveled how overgeneralizing after a phone call had distorted his thinking, affected his communication and his personal and work relationships, and negatively impacted his ability to engage or respond to people in a timely way. He told me that he has hope for things to improve now that texting and emails are replacing phone calls. I thought to myself, *I hope no one gives him bad news in a text.*

Fortune-Telling and Mind Reading

Fortune-telling occurs when we jump to conclusions that don't fit with the facts. This happens when we try to predict the future then act as if our predictions are true. Often our predictions are irrational and unrealistic, but we still hold on to the beliefs. Most of us jump to conclusions at various times in our lives. It can be in small, seemingly insignificant ways, like when we send a note to someone and ask to meet with them but there is no response. We fill the void with fortune-telling: *Perhaps they don't want to meet with me. Maybe they don't like talking with me, or maybe they think I'm a loser. Well, forget it, I don't need their friendship; I'll never talk to them again.*

Bumping into the person at the market a few weeks later, you find out that they didn't receive your note and would happily get together with you. Meanwhile, you have needlessly filled your mind with negative emotions based on your distorted thinking. Disappointment, resentment, sadness, and anger all bubbled around in you until you were willing to end the relationship to ease the pain.

This distortion often occurs when we're faced with uncertainty and our minds cannot tolerate the unknown or the unresolved. The speculation is a way to fill in the gaps with a conclusion that may have no grounding in fact, but at least it fills the gap and we feel a sense of closure. Most of the time the person jumping to conclusions isn't even aware they are doing it. The problems occur because a negative prediction, even if irrational, can lead the person to a self-inflicted defeat. This kind of distorted thinking is commonly used by those who espouse conspiracy theories, drawing sometimes outrageously false conclusions about everyday situations.

Closely related to fortune-telling is mind reading. In its various forms, mind reading is one of the most common distortions of our thinking. When we assume what others are thinking or feeling about us without having solid evidence to back up the assumption, we are mind reading.

Imagine approaching a coworker in the office, and before you can greet her, she turns to the person standing next to her, and they whisper a few words then begin to laugh. You turn away horrified, sure they were talking about you and laughing at you. Returning to your desk, you decide to not speak with either of them again.

It is important to recognize that you may have understood the dynamic perfectly and were justified in your response or you may have misinterpreted their behavior. After all, sometimes people do gossip about coworkers and make jokes behind the person's back.

Problems arise when we respond to our assumptions as if they are true and turn away without validating them. When we engage in mind reading on a regular basis, it can easily become a self-fulfilling prophecy where each encounter adds fuel to the fire of our negative belief: *I knew they didn't like me and are trying to hurt me.*

One simple way to test your assumptions is to simply ask the other person if your conclusion about what they are thinking is accurate. They might guiltily admit it, and perhaps even apologize for being such a jerk. You have then demonstrated confidence and maturity by seeking to understand what really happened.

Another thing they might say, if you ask, is that they had been talking about some skits on *Saturday Night Live*, which they both watched over the weekend, and retelling what happened had reminded them how funny it was. Their laughter had nothing to do with you at all. In this case, you are free from wrong assumptions and negative attitudes, and you might decide that this coming weekend you will be sure to watch *Saturday Night Live*.

Personalization

Personalization is similar to mind reading in that it's a distortion in which we believe that everything others do or say is some kind of direct personal reaction to us. We literally take everything personally. Whenever anything doesn't work out the way we expected, we immediately jump in and take the blame for this misfortune, whether or not we have anything to do with the occurrence. This form of distorted thinking is a major source of anxiety and unhappiness and leads us directly to self-blaming.

We all have disappointments, and we all struggle personally from time to time. The distortion occurs when we treat these inevitable occurrences as the result of or as caused by some character flaw or personal failing on our part.

For example, if you are turned down for a promotion, you automatically assume it was because you weren't good enough at your job, even though there could be many different reasons. Maybe there were budget constraints, or perhaps the boss's nephew applied, or perhaps management thinks so highly of you they want to consider you for an even better position. In reality any number of different things could be behind the decision, but all you see is *I'm not good enough.*

Or suppose you are meeting a friend for coffee, and they not only don't show but don't even text you to let you know they're not coming. Your mind might go straight to the assumption they don't like you anymore and find you too boring to even have coffee with. Or you might assume they like someone else better than you, so they decided to meet the other person, leaving you sitting alone in the Starbucks.

The underlying belief when we personalize is not only *It's all about me,* but more negatively, *It's all my fault* or *There's something wrong with me.* We can easily confuse self-blame with taking responsibility, because on the surface they seem similar. However, it isn't helpful to assume responsibility for circumstances that have nothing to do with us.

———

Everyone has distorted thinking from time to time, so we aren't alone in experiencing it. When Paul writes, "Be transformed by the renewing of your mind" (Rom. 12:2), he shines a light of hope that none of us are prisoners of the way we think. By identifying the distortions we relate to, it is possible to change the way we think, and by doing so discover our lives are being transformed in the process.

6

How to Make Yourself Miserable

If you could kick the person in the pants responsible for most of your trouble, you wouldn't sit for a month. — Theodore Roosevelt

I don't think being miserable is simply an accident or something we stumble into unaware. Misery requires a lot of effort and a good working strategy to really pull off. Some people mistake misery for just being sad, or pouty, or even morose, but those are minor inconveniences compared to really being miserable.

Lest you get the idea that being miserable is only for a select few, you'll be glad to know that misery is an equal-opportunity ailment available regardless of our upbringing or circumstances of life. Whether a person only has a little bit of money, or maybe some money, or even tons of money, their levels of happiness and (on the flip side) misery are about even.

The same can be said about levels of education. More education not only doesn't equal happiness, it may actually hinder it. It might be surprising to know that the smartest people can experience the highest levels of depression. Whether a person is single or married, introvert or extrovert, blonde or brunette (in spite of the old saying "blondes have more fun"), no type of person has an advantage on the happiness meter.

Actually, most misery is earned through practice and hard work, much like playing a musical instrument. I learned this lesson when I was a kid, and the school I attended offered optional music lessons on an instrument of our choice. I was excited, until my parents, using the preemptive strike technique, announced, "No drums!"

I knew I didn't want to lug around a trombone or tuba, and trumpets were a little brassy for my taste. So I chose the saxophone, since it seemed cool and I figured eventually I could play in a garage band if I got good enough. Besides, everyone liked the song "Tequila" by The Champs.

I don't think *disappointed* is a strong enough word to describe how I felt when I came home from school with my instrument case and excitedly opened it to find not a shiny new sax but an old used clarinet. Evidently, my parents figured it would be quieter, and besides, they thought it probably had almost the same fingering so I'd never know the difference.

At this very important time in life, with my self-esteem on the line and my personality taking shape, I learned the secret to making myself miserable: blame! This was just the beginning of a lifelong pattern. Other people, circumstances, the dog, the weather, the neighbor's dog, Satan, Satan's dog if he had one, even God—actually, anyone or anything could be blamed whenever things didn't go as I expected them to.

Now, I didn't know at the time that I was embarking on a lifetime journey to make myself miserable. And I certainly didn't realize the most efficient and effective way to accomplish misery is by blaming whenever possible.

The Blame Game

For me, it started with some pretty basic blaming, like blaming my parents for making me be a dweeb, because girls didn't want to hang around with boys who played clarinet. But soon I had branched out into a whole plethora of excuses that involved pointing to someone else, as if to say my life would have been so good if it weren't for *them*. When "mistakes were made," I made sure I wasn't the one who messed up or let others down.

Before long I began to see that there was no limit to who could be blamed for my misfortune. I was able to deflect blame onto others, so that in time and with practice I never had to take responsibility for anything. Of course, having two brothers and a sister was a bonus, because there was always someone around the house I could blame at any time. Anyone can learn to blame parents, siblings, other dysfunctional family members, negative relationships, coworkers, or even life hardships as the cause of all unhappiness and failure.

It seems a little ironic that blaming helps us feel better about ourselves at the time, because we've shifted responsibility away from ourselves, yet we end up feeling miserable and like our lives are out of control because everything that happens is someone else's fault. Blame can leave us feeling powerless because we hold others responsible for our misfortunes.

Habitual blaming over time perpetuates bitterness, resentment, and powerlessness while keeping us from doing the work to take charge of our lives and our mental, emotional, and spiritual health. When we blame, we end up only hurting ourselves as blaming turns us into prisoners of our own bitterness and resentment. Even if our feelings might be justified, they won't help us become happy, healthy, or successful.

Have you ever wondered what it would be like in hell? C. S. Lewis tells us, "Hell begins with a grumbling mood, always complaining, always blaming others."[1] In his book *The Great Divorce*, Lewis writes about hell and the people his narrator found there, one of whom was Napoleon Bonaparte.

> "The nearest of those old ones is Napoleon. We know that because two chaps made the journey to see him. They'd started long before I came, of course, but I was there when they came back. . . ."
>
> "But they got there?"
>
> "That's right. He'd built himself a huge house all in the Empire style—rows of windows flaming with light. . . . They went up and looked through one of the windows. Napoleon was there alright."
>
> "What was he doing?"
>
> "Walking up and down—up and down all the time—left-right, left-right—never stopping for a moment. The two chaps watched him for about a year and he never rested. And muttering to himself all the time. 'It was Soult's fault. It was Ney's fault. It was Josephine's fault. It was the fault of the Russians. It was the fault of the English.' Like that all the time. Never stopped for a moment. A little, fat man and he looked kind of tired. But he didn't seem able to stop it."[2]

Evidently, Napoleon also discovered the secret of how to make himself miserable for all eternity. This brings us to an important issue: Why do we blame? It's easy to see that we do, but why? I think we have some pretty good reasons.

Why Do We Blame?

1. *Blaming is a way to explain why something happened.* It's natural for us to look for reasons and causes for the fortune and misfortune in our lives. Blaming is a quick way to explain why things turned out the way they did, simultaneously diminishing the other person's standing and building up our own status in others' perceptions.

2. *Blaming others is easy, and we're lazy.* Blaming means less work for us, because when we blame, we don't have to be held accountable, thus we don't have to do the hard work of taking responsibility and fixing the problem.

3. *Blaming others keeps up the illusion that we are in control.* Not blaming someone else means we have to accept the notion that perhaps we didn't do everything right, which implies we were out of control. But by blaming someone we get to control the story, showing they were bad and we were good, and since it's all their fault we are free to walk away with our ego intact. Mission accomplished!

4. *Blaming is a way to attack someone who has hurt us in the past. Or anyone.* When we go into attack mode, blaming is a perfect weapon. If we wield it effectively, it can be a lethal way to try to hurt those who are close to us. A side benefit is that if they try to deny they are at fault and belatedly attempt to shift the blame back

to us, it only makes them seem weak and defensive. We win either way.

5. *It's a great defense mechanism.* Blame is a great way to preserve our sense of self-esteem by distracting everyone's attention to the failings of the blamee, thus keeping people unaware of our own failures and flaws.

Of course, blaming didn't start with us; there are examples of folks blaming others and making themselves miserable all through the Bible. We can go all the way back to the garden of Eden to see how it all began. After disobeying God, Adam and Eve hid in the bushes and immediately started blaming. Eve blamed the serpent for deceiving her. Adam initially blamed Eve for giving him the fruit in the first place, then blamed God for "the woman you put here with me" (Gen. 3:12). So, it wasn't Adam's fault, it wasn't Eve's fault—it was God's fault for creating Eve, who then would give Adam the fruit. We've been shifting the blame ever since.

In ancient Israel's history, there is reference to a scapegoat.

> He shall take the two goats and present them before the LORD at the doorway of the tent of meeting. Aaron shall cast lots for the two goats, one lot for the LORD and the other lot for the scapegoat. Then Aaron shall offer the goat on which the lot for the LORD fell and make it a sin offering. But the goat on which the lot for the scapegoat fell shall be presented alive before the LORD, to make atonement upon it, to send it into the wilderness as the scapegoat. (Lev. 16:7–10 NASB)

All the sins and transgressions of the people were to be confessed, then placed on the head of the goat, which was then released into the wilderness to bear the guilt of the people. As Dwight D. Eisenhower said, "The search for a scapegoat is the easiest of all hunting expeditions."[3]

In 1871, the Great Chicago Fire burned for three days, killing almost three hundred people. No sooner had the fire been extinguished than a search for a scapegoat started. The *Chicago Tribune* reported that the fire began when a cow being milked by Catherine O'Leary kicked over a kerosene lamp, setting fire to her barn. The reporter admitted years later that he made it up. (Mrs. O'Leary was sleeping when the fire started.)

Finding someone to blame was a priority—preferably someone who couldn't fight back. Mrs. O'Leary, both a woman and of Irish heritage (two groups that were marginalized at the time), was an easy target for placing the blame.

"All blame is a waste of time," Wayne Dyer writes.

No matter how much fault you find with another, and regardless of how much you blame him, it will not change you. The only thing blame does is to keep the focus off you when you are looking for external reasons to explain your unhappiness or frustration. You may succeed in making another feel guilty about something by blaming him, but you won't succeed in changing whatever it is about you that is making you unhappy.[4]

Blaming is like a two-sided coin. One side is "It's not my fault," and the flip side is "It's all my fault!" Either will stunt our personal growth and keep us from experiencing the freedom that comes from taking responsibility for our actions. Every person will be wrong sometimes. Mistakes are made every minute of every day, and yet we still find it difficult to admit when we are the one to blame, we are the guilty person, or we are wrong.

Now, I admit it, I hate being wrong! And to make it even worse, I've spent a lot of my life looking for a way out by blaming others, circumstances, the weather, the dark side (and the Force), parents, teachers, the system, and The Man.

Sometimes I was absolutely right and it was someone else's fault. But along the way, while attempting to take attention away from myself, I developed a pattern of defensiveness that hurt relationships, created unnecessary conflicts, and made me difficult to be around.

At an early age, I discovered the lethal combination of being smart and verbal. That can be a good mix when used in a positive, healthy, constructive way. However, too often I was attempting to manipulate those around me so that I could always appear right even when I knew I was wrong. I became the person described as, "He's not always right, but he's never in doubt."

One day a friend looked me in the eye and told me, "You can be right or you can be healthy, but you can't be both." I knew I had to change.

Most of the time I wasn't even conscious of what I was doing; it had become habitual, and seemed almost natural for me to act this way. I found myself making more mistakes in my new attempts to own up to my mistakes. At first, in trying to take responsibility for myself, I swung to the opposite pole and assumed I was at fault for everything, even if it had nothing to do with me. I suppose the same personal insecurity that demanded I appear right was now demanding I appear wrong. They are just two sides of the same dysfunction.

When we are wrong, we have a choice: admit the mistake or try to hide it in hopes that no one notices. It may seem easy and appropriate to simply admit we were wrong and accept whatever consequences may come. But as humans, we are more prone to not admit fault even when we know we were wrong—and everyone else does too.

Telling the truth, especially when we are wrong, makes us better people. Trust grows in a relationship when we admit we are wrong. When we are in a relationship with someone and we have to be right, even when we know we are wrong, the relationship erodes and eventually we will destroy all that person's trust. However, when we admit we are wrong, trust increases, and the other person sees us as someone they could approach, which can open the door for them to be honest and admit they are sometimes wrong too.

In hindsight, I realize I grew up believing that admitting I was wrong was a sign of weakness. But my insistence on being right, even when I was stupidly wrong, was the real weakness. Admitting mistakes actually shows strength and courage. Not admitting my mistakes led me to be on the lookout for someone to fault. Anybody but me. Finding fault inevitably undermines relationships, and we look like cowards.

Why Is It So Hard to Admit We Are Wrong?

When we begin to own our mistakes, positive things happen. As long as we hide or cover up our mistakes, we'll continue to make the same mistakes over and over again. But admitting we are wrong opens the possibility of addressing the problem, correcting the mistake, and greatly increasing our chances of not making the same mistake again and again.

As people see you are being honest and sincerely trying to learn from your mistakes, their respect for you will grow. It takes courage to say, "I was wrong and I'm sorry." It is inevitable that you will be wrong in your life. Owning responsibility allows others to see your strongest self.

How we say "I'm sorry" will have a big impact on the other person's response. Some apologies are so muddled that they aren't apologies at all. Some are vague without owning responsibility for the actual problem. Others are specific and clear, and those apologies can result in acceptance and growth.

Accepting responsibility is the first step in rebuilding trust. When this is followed by the second step, an offer to fix the damage or remedy the situation, it is even more effective. The third step is to explain the mistake, which helps build understanding of the issue. The second and third steps lose their helpfulness if the first step of accepting responsibility isn't accomplished.

Sometimes we jump straight to explaining the situation that led to the mistake without accepting responsibility; this is rightly seen as self-justification, not a real apology.

Part of why it's hard to admit we are wrong, even in the face of mounting evidence against us, is the way our brain processes information. We all have biases for how we receive and use information. This is called *cognitive bias*.

We have learned and accepted ideas throughout our lives that help us understand the world around us and how we relate to it. We are often not aware of these biases, but they enable us to sort information according to whether it aligns with our present way of thinking. Ideas that are contrary to our mindset are easily dismissed so that we can maintain an unconflicted view of the world.

The process by which we screen information is called *selective perception*. This is the dynamic of receiving and accepting information that supports and aligns with what we already believe to be true. Likewise, it rejects ideas and information that contradict or undermine our current beliefs. Selective perception is not a bad thing; it is merely a way our brains work to help us remain stable in the face of overwhelming and often conflicting information.

When We Need to Be Right

We all have a choice to make. Do you want to be right or do you want to be healthy? If we always need to be right, we will never be healthy. The downside of having to be right is that we will stand unmoved even while we experience deteriorating physical and emotional health. Studies show that people who maintain their "rightness" often find themselves suffering from ulcers, high blood pressure, dysfunctional relationships, and high levels of stress.[5]

In addition to causing physical damage, this "rightness" also undermines relationships and often leaves us isolated. We cling to our belief or opinion with the same tenacity that Gollum clung to his precious ring in the Lord of the Rings series.

Of course, there are often times we are right. That is not the same as needing to be right or trying to show that others with differing opinions, experiences, and insights are wrong. Where does this irritating habit come from? We might have learned that we weren't rewarded, considered, or loved when we were wrong. That observation in a young child gets reinforced when they hear parents or other adults fiercely standing their ground through shouting or demeaning arguments.

The good news is that when we don't have to be right, we no longer need to stand our ground, insisting we are right and others are wrong. Letting go of blame doesn't sugarcoat unfair circumstances, nor does it excuse hurtful people or gloss over the very real hardships we go through in life. But it does free us to see the situation clearly and work toward solutions that are helpful. When we choose to let go of blaming behavior, we become empowered to see reality and make choices that are helpful and healthy.

"People are always blaming their circumstances for what they are," said George Bernard Shaw. "I don't believe in circumstances. The people who get on in this world are the people who get up and look for circumstances they want, and, if they can't find them, make them."[6]

Self-blame is also destructive, so the answer lies not in blaming ourselves but in taking responsibility without blame. Taking away the blame without removing the responsibility keeps us accountable to ourselves and those around us without setting us up for shame and guilt. We don't get to be right; in fact, we get to be wrong with dignity, authenticity, and ownership that are the opposite of self-abuse.

What We Lose When We Blame

Blaming others has significant implications for our personal life and relationships. Some of the losses we may experience include:

- *Personal growth.* When we spend our time constantly defending ourselves and pointing out who is to blame, we tend to push people away, cutting ourselves off from the good things others have to offer us in terms of lessons and growth. As we become increasingly closed off to input from others, our defensiveness can turn to anger and resentment that further isolate us.

- *Our power.* By making everything everyone else's fault, we actually end up making ourselves seem powerless. This is logical, because if everything is someone else's fault then it means we don't have the power to change anything, because others are really in charge.

- *Healthy relationships.* If we are blamers, it's likely we won't be able to maintain strong relationships with others. Blaming others is a way of putting people down, so it is also a way to push people away. Our blaming can create a dangerous environment where there is no trust and people can't relax around us because they might feel judged and demeaned.

- *Positive influence on others.* Blame can be contagious. When we blame, people around us are also more likely to turn and blame others for things. Like the spread of a virus, we may not even be aware that we are infecting those around us with our tendency to avoid responsibility by blaming. Not only are we having a negative impact on others but we are also hurting ourselves. Soon, we come to realize the more we blame, the more miserable our lives become.

Paul reminds us that everyone who judges—and blaming is certainly judging others—has no excuse. "For in passing judgment on another you condemn yourself, because you, the judge, practice the very same things" (Rom. 2:1 ESV). By putting blame on others, we are, in effect, trying to build ourselves up. "Look what they did!" can be translated, "I'm so much better than they are!" Meanwhile, we avoid accepting responsibility for our actions or lack of action, shifting all negativity onto other people.

It's not easy to stop blaming and accept personal responsibility. There are always books and articles telling us to just quit it and just do it. These may be well-meaning, but honestly, changing behavior that is ingrained into our minds by years of hard-earned experience will not simply happen because of our good intentions. But difficult doesn't mean impossible, and there is no other way to move away from misery.

"My mother abandoned me when I was just eight," actor Hugh Jackman shared. "There comes a certain point in life, when you have to stop blaming other people for how you feel or misfortunes in your life. You can't go through life obsessing about what might have been."[7]

What has taken us years to develop will not change in an instant. It will require a plan of action that leads us out of our self-made misery into a life of realistic joy. When Jesus asked the disabled man at the pool in John 5:6, "Do you want to get well?" it was a fairly straightforward question. Instead of answering Jesus's question, however, the man responded by blaming others who had people to assist them, blaming those who didn't help him, and blaming the unfair system that only let healing come to the quickest responders.

Jesus didn't bat an eye and told the man to pick up his mat and walk (v. 8). I wonder if after thirty-eight years of sitting by the pool, imagining what it would be like to have his turn in the water and feel the bubbles work their magic and strengthen his legs, then emerging from the water whole and strong while the crowd cheered and celebrated his miraculous healing, the man might have found Jesus's words to be a great disappointment. *Just pick up my mat and walk away? Is that all?*

It's no surprise that when he walked off and was confronted by the authorities for working on the Sabbath by carrying his mat, he went right back to his old, miserable habits and blamed someone else. He told them that the person to blame was the man who healed him, because he'd told him to pick up his mat and walk! It wasn't his fault nor his responsibility; after all, he was the victim here. When they asked who was to blame, he didn't even know who had healed him. Jesus was just someone new to blame.

Are we very different? Do we stay with our old behaviors even when God wants to answer our prayers? If we were given the desires of our hearts, would we fall back into old habits? Or can we choose to stop blaming others and circumstances in order to live with healthy personal responsibility?

How to Accept Responsibility

I was going to write more about how to stop blaming others, but the more important issue is how to take responsibility for our actions, choices, mistakes, and successes. When we start taking responsibility in healthy ways, our blaming behavior will fade away.

The first step to responsible living is accepting that our own actions may have led us to the situation we're in now, whether we like it or not. This makes it easier to apologize when we have done something wrong or let others down. The most significant new habit we can develop is apologizing as fast as is humanly possible. Don't wait until others have proven you are to blame; that just turns them into blamers. If you apologize quickly and sincerely, it will catch people off guard, and sometimes it will confuse them because they are prepared for your usual arguments and excuses. Saying "I'm sorry" undermines years of predictable power struggles and defensiveness.

One of the first worship services I led at a church in Seattle taught me this lesson. My fellow pastor Ray Moore was speaking and mentioned how his wife, Judy, often looked up things in a dictionary she carried around with her, which seemed innocent enough. But suddenly a woman who looked like a street person, which isn't at all unusual in Seattle, interrupted the service as she ran down the aisle carrying a stack of books in her arms while twelve hundred people looked on.

We were shocked into silence. As the lady approached the front of the sanctuary, she began to scream, "I demand an apology! I demand an apology!" While she continued screaming, I was looking around to see where all the ushers had disappeared to. Then I wondered if I was expected to deal with this person since I was obviously the new guy on the pastoral team. Remarkably, Ray kept his cool. Looking at the woman, he asked, "Do you want me to apologize?"

"Yeeesss! I want an apology," she wailed.

"All right, then, I apologize to you. I'm sorry."

Suddenly turning, the lady ran back out of the sanctuary, screaming, still carrying her stack of books. I looked over at Ray, wondering if this was some kind of staged sermon illustration, which some churches are known to do, using trained actors from the congregation. He just shrugged and went on with his message.

That morning I learned the power of a fast apology. After the service, I asked Ray why he'd apologized so quickly, even though he hadn't done anything wrong. He said that what mattered to him was that, for whatever reason, the woman felt hurt and wounded and needed someone to apologize to her. He smiled and said, "I don't mind being the one to give her what she thought she needed. And I figured the sooner I did it, the better for all of us."

When we step up and accept responsibility, it isn't just for the bad stuff. Realizing we are responsible for the good and bad that happens opens the door to celebrate the positive results of our actions. Our self-esteem grows in a healthy way, and we don't feel like whatever happens is because of someone else. Affirmations and recognition of our achievements are deserved and humbly received.

When we follow through on promises and commitments, others recognize us as people who are true to their word and can be trusted. This requires us to be realistic, to sometimes say no, and to only make commitments we want or intend to fulfill.

As we begin to change from passive behavior—such as blaming others, making excuses, and bemoaning our situation—to personal responsibility, we become people of action. The action may involve needing to apologize, fix the problem, or plan the steps that lead to meeting our next challenge. Taking action is a significant part of living responsibly.

Finally, we must remember that no one is perfect, including ourselves, and it is imperative to learn and practice forgiving ourselves. Mistakes don't make us bad people; mistakes are lessons we can use to become better people going forward. Kindness is for ourselves as well as for others.

Why Am I Worrying about Worrying?

Anxiety is the dizziness of freedom. — Søren Kierkegaard

Not long ago I received a birthday card from a friend that showed a newspaper clipping. "The world is too big for us," it read,

> too much is going on, too many crimes, too much violence and excitement. Try as you will, you get behind in the race in spite of yourself. It's a constant strain to keep pace, and still you lose ground. Science empties its discoveries on you so fast that you stagger beneath them in hopeless bewilderment. The political world is news seen rapidly. You are out of breath trying to keep pace with who's in and who's out. Everything is high pressure. Human nature cannot endure much more.

This clipping was from the *Atlantic Journal*, June 16, 1883.

It took me a moment to realize it was written so long ago; it could just as well apply to our lives today. Stress and the anxiety that often accompanies it are as much a part of daily living as breathing and walking. Yet we are certainly not the first generation to feel pressure and wonder at the pace of life and the burdens and opportunities that we face daily.

I've never thought of myself as an anxious person. Sure, my life has been impacted by anxiety, as many of the people closest to me have struggled with anxiety, worry, panic attacks, and trauma for years. But the other night, Eileen casually asked if I was worried or stressed about something we were dealing with. I reminded her that I'm not a worrier, and rather than getting anxious, I just get depressed. It seemed to make sense to me at the time.

But in the process of researching and writing this chapter, I began to rethink things. The more I learned about the characteristics of men and women who experience high-functioning anxiety, the more I saw myself on those pages.

Could it be that throughout my life, the troubling issues that surfaced repeatedly, which I chalked up to personality quirks, were actually traits of an anxiety disorder? The many times I drove my family and coworkers crazy with idiosyncrasies and behavior that often put more stress on them might have been my problem all along.

Perhaps I didn't recognize or diagnose my issues because high-functioning anxiety is a form of anxiety disorder that appears very different on the surface. People who experience it are often very successful; they tend to be well dressed and appear overtly calm and in control. Leaning toward perfectionism, they push themselves and those around them to perform to the limit.

An aspect of this is that people like me come to depend on the anxiety experience to energize us to accomplish our goals. While many people are immobilized by anxiety, those with high-functioning anxiety often become driven in such a way that it doesn't hold them back in readily apparent ways. Below the surface, though, is the insidious undercurrent of worrying about worrying and being anxious about being anxious. "Worrying is carrying tomorrow's load with today's strength—carrying two days at once," says Corrie ten Boom. "It is moving into tomorrow ahead of time. Worrying doesn't empty tomorrow of its sorrow, it empties today of its strength."[1]

Under the Surface

Appearances are not always what they seem. When we left our home in Seattle and moved to the Bay Area in California, we decided to put our house on the rental market until we were able to sell it. We quickly found good tenants, and my friend Tom offered to keep an eye on it for us.

It wasn't very long before I got a letter from Tom with a clipping from a newspaper showing the front of our house. The article told about the family now living in our house. Evidently, while backing a moving truck into the driveway, they plowed into a fire hydrant near the corner of our property. The hydrant broke and shot plumes of water high into the air, actually going over the roof of our house and flooding the neighbors on the other side.

A fire truck came, and the firefighters set to work capping the upper part of the hydrant. Water was evidently still coming out, so they checked and realized that the hydrant had also broken off below ground, so they also repaired that damage.

After things calmed down and the firefighters returned to their station, the family went inside and ate their first dinner in their new home. But they soon began to hear popping sounds. Looking out the window, they couldn't see anything wrong.

Suddenly, the concrete driveway beneath the moving truck broke apart, revealing that an underground cavern had been created by the water from the hydrant. The resulting sinkhole swallowed the truck, essentially burying it in what remained of our driveway.

Taking a closer look at the picture in the news article, I thought about how our lives may seem perfectly stable on the surface. When problems arise, we handle them and move forward, with very little trouble. The danger is that below the surface, our foundations may be eroding, and soon we too will hear popping noises as our lives suddenly crash in a way we never foresaw.

In all our lives, there is damage below the surface where no one can see it. We carry guilt, feel pain, and hide our secrets, moving along as if everything is all right. Until, without warning, it all falls apart.

Those with high-functioning anxiety often find it difficult to back away or give up on circumstances or people, which can cause us to remain in toxic relationships and poisoned environments way past normal limits—causing more under-the-surface damage. Throughout my career, I found it nearly impossible to encourage a disruptive staff member to find a new place to work that might be a better fit for them, even when they seemed to be begging me to fire them.

Maybe I couldn't believe they wouldn't come around to my way of thinking eventually. Besides, I wanted to be liked by everyone, which can lead to ineffective, people-pleasing behavior. People with high-functioning anxiety often spend time trying to figure out what others want or expect from them, then perform in ways that hopefully win approval. Evidently, we'll do so even if it is a futile effort.

Another common characteristic of people with high-functioning anxiety is procrastination. Others don't recognize that procrastination is an issue because the person performs at a high level and often achieves a great deal. Looks can be deceiving. Just because someone appears successful (and maybe is successful) doesn't mean that procrastination isn't a looming issue for them.

I've struggled with procrastination most of my life. Whether it has held me back or not, I don't really know, but I know it has driven the people nearest me, family and coworkers alike, completely bonkers. I've carried guilt and remorse and maybe a little bit of shame for being a procrastinator, and lots of people far smarter than I have given their best efforts to try to fix me.

Perfect Storm of Procrastination

As someone who has ADHD, I find it easy to become distracted, lose my focus, and get off track when interruptions, opportunities, obstacles, or setbacks cause me to do stupid things. Even with good preparation and the best of intentions, life can get messy in a hurry.

While I was pastoring a startup church in Seattle, there were always things that needed to be done but not very many folks to do them. But to help me stay focused on what was most important, I established a routine for Sunday mornings. I always got to the church early so I'd have plenty of time to prepare myself for worship and preaching.

One Sunday on my way to church, I stopped at the supermarket to pick up the donuts, fruit, and bagels we would serve after the worship time. Arriving at the church, I went into my office and sat at my desk, intending to pray, review my sermon notes, and focus my thoughts on what was to come.

Suddenly I had an idea to check the restrooms to make sure there were paper towels. I knew someone in the Friday night AA group habitually took our paper towels, leaving none for our Sunday morning folks. Sure enough, I checked the men's restroom and there were no paper towels. I figured I had better check the women's restroom just to be thorough, and of course, no paper towels there, and no toilet paper either. So I restocked the restrooms then for good measure also refilled the soap dispensers. Satisfied that I had taken care of a potential crisis in the restrooms, I headed back to my office to prepare for worship.

As I stepped into my office, I noticed that just inside the doorway a light in the ceiling had burned out. Well, I couldn't have that. How could I focus properly with a burned-out ceiling light? I got a ladder and a new bulb from the storage closet and changed the bulb so now I'd have good lighting for my prep time. While carrying the ladder back to its place in the storage closet, I happened to glance over by the stairway and saw another burned-out light. I knew it wasn't safe to have a light out on the stairwell, so I carried the ladder over and replaced that bulb as well.

I set the ladder aside and started walking back toward my office, but then I noticed another light out by the women's restroom, where I had just replenished the paper towels, toilet paper, and soap. Thinking it would be terrible if someone stumbled while leaving the women's restroom because of my negligence, I changed that bulb as well.

Carrying the ladder back to the storage closet again, I was now alert enough to spot another dead light bulb near the entrance to the sanctuary, so I quickly changed it, as well as another one over the refreshment table.

I did it! Five dead light bulbs and I fixed them all. Feeling a little bit proud for having accomplished something, I finally put the ladder away and sat down at my desk to prepare myself for worship.

While glancing over my sermon notes, I thought perhaps I should make coffee, not only for myself but also for worshipers who would desperately want their coffee when they arrived. After all, it's a requirement in Seattle, and it has to be Starbucks!

It would only take a second, so I went into the kitchen, made the coffee, then thought, *As long as I'm already here, I may as well cut up the fruit and put it on serving trays.*

Just then some people arrived, so I greeted them. I was chatting with them when I had the idea, *Why not multitask—since I'm already standing here talking with these people, I may as well cut the bagels and get them out, along with the donuts.* Did I mention that the number one cause of household injuries in the United States is cutting bagels? After I nicked my finger with the serrated knife, I got the first aid kit and bandaged my bleeding finger. Then, while setting everything out on the tables, I noticed I had forgotten to get out the cream cheese, and people were definitely going to want cream cheese with their perfectly cut bagels.

While getting the bowl of cream cheese, I couldn't help noticing that the church was beginning to fill up as more people kept arriving. It was time for the service to begin. I went back to my office, gathered up my stuff, and walked out to lead worship.

I had planned to pray, focus, and prepare—and instead I spent the morning chasing after insignificant stuff. I was distracted, busy, and not on task. I realized how easy it is, even with good intentions and a desire to focus on the important things, to veer off track, believing that as soon as I took care of the little things I'd be able to give my undivided attention to the important issues.

Since then, I've bought the self-help books, read articles, and talked with life coaches, to no avail. I'll save you some time and money right now by telling you why most books and advice about procrastination don't work and will never help you get over it: there is a fundamental misunderstanding in our culture about the nature and causes of procrastination, and thus none of the advice is right or helpful.

Most attempts to fix a procrastinator start with the premise that the root problem is a lack of organization. They work to get people to be more organized, be tidy, and utilize various time management tools. Every clean freak thinks they can help the poor procrastinator. If you just try harder to make lists, put things in boxes, fill in your calendar, and manage your time better, everything will be done in a crisp and clean way, end of problem. Wrong!

Those of us who have difficulty getting around to doing certain things realize no amount of organizing or time management will help us do those particular tasks. They'll get done eventually, usually in desperation at the absolute last minute, or perhaps by someone else, but it's not because we are disorganized.

Procrastination is rooted in our avoidance of unpleasant feelings. When we feel uncomfortable about some task, it will be set aside for as long as humanly possible. If we think there is a strong possibility that we might fail, or at least do a poor job of it, we will stall and delay as long as we can get away with it. Sometimes, much to our relief, someone sees what's not being done, and since it isn't something that makes them uncomfortable, they jump in and do it for us.

Unfortunately, the sad truth is that those very things we avoid and delay, because of fear that we might fail, are often the most important things we have to accomplish. If they were small, insignificant tasks, we wouldn't procrastinate, because there is no worry about how we'll do. Perhaps this explains why, when facing a huge project deadline, we procrastinators will accomplish more things than anyone thought humanly possible—often everything and anything except the big, looming job that matters most.

When we feel bad about an impending task, we are more likely to procrastinate in an attempt to feel better. And we may succeed at feeling better in the moment, but the cost of feeling bad merely gets pushed onto our future self.

Those of us who experience anxiety, in the form of either worrying about the future or ruminating on the past, can be more prone to procrastination. Similarly, depression has been shown to correlate with procrastination. So, I guess my brain is a perfect storm.

Because those with high-functioning anxiety set the standard quite high, we often recoil from doing anything where we may fail and disappoint everyone. In our viewpoint, it is better to not try than to try and fail to achieve the goal. Like a duck that looks peaceful and serene floating on the surface of a pond but is paddling like crazy under the water, we may seem successful at school, work, or home, but there is a lot of action going on under the surface.

Boston clinical psychologist Inna Khazan observes that while everything appears fine on the outside, people with high-functioning anxiety are, on the inside, "experiencing a near-constant state of anxiety." She says, "People with high-functioning anxiety push themselves to get things done, with anxiety constantly holding a 'stick' over their heads. . . . Fear of what might happen if they don't move forward keeps them moving forward. And because these people are often high-achieving, no one thinks that there is anything 'wrong' with them."[2]

While it may be true that what we tell ourselves impacts how we feel and the decisions we make, we can change the way we think and begin to feel differently. It is possible to train our brains to think differently. This means we are not stuck with pessimistic thinking or unhealthy attitudes. We don't have to be held back by doubt, self-criticism, or catastrophic thinking. Assuming *I'm such an idiot* or *This will never work* or *No one will ever love me* can easily turn into self-fulfilling prophecies.

Don't worry about success. We only see success in the rear-view mirror. We look back and realize something succeeded, but we rarely notice it at the time we are doing it. Besides, success is never guaranteed. We can, however, take steps forward and achieve important goals that in time will add up to success.

Signs of High-Functioning Anxiety

"A person who experiences functional anxiety remains able to move through daily activities without the burden of constant, severe anxiety," says clinical psychologist Carla Marie Manly.

As such, an individual with functional anxiety may function and engage in life activities without the effects of anxiety being highly obvious. In fact, a person with functional anxiety may appear to be very calm. However, a person living with functional anxiety often finds that anxiety "leaks out" in the form of nervous tics, perfectionism, and overachievement or controlling habits.[3]

Someone with high-functioning anxiety often does or experiences the following:

1. *Pays close attention to details.* Structure reduces anxiety. When someone feels that things are starting to spin out of control, it is a natural response to create structure to help him or her feel stabilized. Any action that might be perceived as risky will be avoided as anxiety increases. Roller coasters and scary movies can seem thrilling and fun to some people, but the person with high-functioning anxiety is not thrilled with the idea of these.

   Preoccupation with safety can lead to hypervigilance and a desire to withdraw in order to preserve safety. When a possible threat is undefined or unknown, the uncertainty of its timing, intensity, and frequency brings a general feeling of apprehension. The fear of the unknown makes people preoccupied.

   By focusing on details, organizing, strategizing, and working to make things as perfect as possible, they can achieve a sense of orderliness and control. This is essential, because the anxious person often feels out of control. Even controlling little details can give a small sense of stability and certainty in an uncertain world.

2. *Can't sleep.* Internalizing anxiety can help us get
   through the day, but anxiety often shows itself in the
   form of sleep disturbance. Having trouble going to
   sleep, waking during the night, and having trouble getting back to sleep can be a sign that the anxiety below
   the surface is finding a way to assert itself. Another
   manifestation of this issue occurs when a person's sleep
   cycle changes unexpectedly. People may find themselves
   barely able to wake up or stay awake during the day,
   then suddenly become night creatures, staying alert and
   awake throughout the night.

3. *Focuses on control.* Those of us with high-functioning
   anxiety want to feel as if we are in charge of life, which
   can lead to unconscious controlling actions. These actions allow us to feel more in control of events or outcomes than we actually are. Because of our anxious inter-
   nal feelings, we may not see ourselves as very controlling,
   while people around us often view us as control freaks.

   My friend Randy and I were talking about our different leadership styles, and he explained to me that
   he doesn't worry about the final outcomes but is me-
   ticulously controlling about the steps to get there. I
   told him I was just the opposite. I only care about the
   final outcome, and I'm completely indifferent to how
   we get there. We looked at each other in wonder that,
   with such big differences, we are both controllers yet we
   didn't worry about the same things.

4. *Is unable to relax.* The inability to relax takes many
   forms. It could be staying busy with work-related
   projects, tasks at home, even compulsive exercise, but
   it leaves us unable to have downtime. This can also

take the form of striving for perfection in ourselves and those around us. Unrealistic expectations about achievements or appearance are a common expression of high-functioning anxiety. The tension can reveal itself in our physical health as well. Neck aches, shoulder pain, and a knot in the stomach are signals that the body is adversely affected by anxiety. Nervous habits like biting nails, picking, or rhythmically twitching or moving are often unconscious ways to deal with the underlying tension.

5. *Pushes to the limits.* Often people with high-functioning anxiety push themselves beyond what might be considered normal limits. Extraordinary effort is expended even when the person is exhausted and depleted emotionally and physically. The greater problem is not what they do to themselves but the way they push family, friends, and coworkers past reasonable limits as well. Those who are being pushed can feel like it is abusive and demanding, fueling resentment and anger that can damage relationships and work environments. Sometimes the anxious person finds it nearly impossible to back off.

6. *Plans everything.* The best chess players know that a key strategy is planning several moves ahead. This is also a characteristic of people with high-functioning anxiety. Planning into the future is a way to manage their symptoms. The unknown is seen as a threat, so the more that can be known and anticipated, the fewer unknowns there are to take them by surprise.

This planning and refining of plans is a common trait and includes both positive planning and preparing for every possible negative outcome. The ability to assess resistance, defeat, and potential failure is often a by-product of anxious feelings. Perhaps we think that by identifying every possible bad thing that could happen, we will be able to ultimately overcome them and succeed in spite of obstacles.

Benefits of Anxiety

People who live with anxiety know that it can be exhausting, painful, and frustrating. Its symptoms can rob us of sleep, joy, confidence, and peace of mind. In unexpected ways, however, anxiety can be a good thing in our lives, in that it can help us recognize and unleash some of our most significant strengths and abilities.

A person who tends to be anxious may also be highly intelligent. Researchers, critical thinkers, analyzers, and tech gurus are often anxiety-prone. As we come to understand our anxiety experience, it can help us learn to explore options and problem-solve adeptly. This, in turn, improves our mental and emotional intelligence.

Anxiety can also serve as a GPS to identify what needs to be addressed in our lives. If a situation or a thought keeps causing anxiety, it may be a signal of something that needs our primary attention. Anxiety in this way can direct us to things or situations that are too important to ignore.

Feelings of fear are intended to keep us safe from danger and threats. Anxious feelings can serve to alert us to potential threats that we might otherwise ignore. It's been said that just because you are paranoid doesn't mean they aren't out to get you. Anxiety sometimes signals a warning that our fears are in fact true, in order to protect us from very real threats. As we learn to pay attention to our anxious feelings, this allows us to assess whether there really is danger and how best to care for ourselves.

For many people, anxiety fuels overachievement and incessant action. For many others, it is the opposite. Anxiety leaves these people feeling paralyzed, unable to take action, and helpless to move forward. But the energy fueling anxious thoughts is available to empower us to get unstuck and act where needed. When this energy is kept bottled up, our minds spin in circles and our bodies fidget or panic. When we use the energy to take action, it reduces the pressure and empowers us in positive ways.

I'm Doing It Anyway!

Whether our anxiety helps us or holds us back depends to a large extent on how we think about it. Often it is our anxiety about having anxiety in the first place that causes so many difficulties. "Negative beliefs, or worrying about worrying, add to your anxiety and keep worry going," writes psychologist Jeffrey Bernstein.

> When people feel controlled by their anxiety they often accept their anxious talk as their destiny. If, however, you challenge your anxiety with the phrase, "I'm doing it anyway" then you will likely find yourself in a better place. This phrase will influence you to take action and create a new reality that is no longer confined by your anxiety.[4]

When we follow Dr. Bernstein's insight, our response changes from debilitating anxiety to positive action. We can tell ourselves,

I really don't want to study tonight because I think I will bomb this test, but I'm studying anyway. Or, I feel so rejected and humiliated because he broke up with me. A big part of me wants to stay home and not go to this party, but I'm going anyway.

As an experiment, I'm going to embrace saying, "I'm doing it anyway," and use this powerful tool to talk back to my own anxiety and stop it from inhibiting me. Because life is too short to worry about worrying.

8

Living beyond Past Trauma

Anything that is human is mentionable, and anything that is mentionable can be more manageable. When we can talk about our feelings, they become less overwhelming, less upsetting, and less scary. — Fred Rogers

We all have some traumatic memories, which could include devastating experiences like a car accident or a house fire; natural disasters such as earthquakes, floods, and hurricanes; rape or other sexual abuse; a violent parent, an addicted spouse, a medical emergency, or assault; as well as the horrors of war. These types of experiences are more common than we might suppose.

While trauma related to natural disasters can be debilitating, man-made traumas are sometimes more difficult to deal with. This can be because the perpetrators might still live near their victims or are family members, providing reminders of the past as well as remaining a threat of further incidents.

Sometimes it is hard for other people to grasp what trauma victims go through. "People think because you have PTSD, you're a pariah or something," said actress Abigail Breslin. "It can come across as maybe scary or frightening to other people, but when you're in those flashbacks or states, it's twice as hard to keep it in. I hope people keep an open mind about it."[1]

Breslin, who was nominated for an Academy Award for her role in *Little Miss Sunshine*, shared her private battle with post-traumatic stress disorder (PTSD), which developed after she experienced sexual assault and domestic violence. In an emotional Instagram post, she wrote, "It's not the same for everybody, and people who deal with it have to deal with it every day."[2]

Not all such memories cause people to experience trauma later in life, but they do cause problems for many, and for some it is debilitating. Trauma can affect us in the long-term mentally, emotionally, physically, and spiritually. Mental responses can include memory problems, lack of concentration, poor judgment, and difficulty making decisions. Emotional issues can include depression, withdrawal, flashbacks, excitability, intense fear, feelings of helplessness, feeling out of control, loss of meaning, and feeling disconnected.

Physically, people in trauma might experience stomach pains, tightness of the chest, headaches, Irritable Bowel Syndrome (IBS), sweating, and psychosomatic complaints. Behavioral responses can include irritability, jumpiness, insomnia, and communication difficulties, as well as drug, nicotine, and alcohol abuse.

People with PTSD can become hypersensitive, with nerves on a permanent state of high alert. Fear and anxiety can recur without warning; nightmares and flashbacks can be torturous. In addition, abuse victims often feel humiliated, vulnerable, helpless, and out of control.

In her book *Trauma and Recovery*, Judith Lewis Herman observes, "The conflict between the will to deny horrible events and the will to proclaim them aloud is the central dialectic of psychological trauma."[3] She adds that post-traumatic stress commonly shows itself in three distinct ways:

- First, hyperarousal arises from continual vigilance in hopes that the experience will not occur again.
- Second, the traumatic memory is constantly in the mind of the traumatized. The memory repeatedly occurs as a flashback, which can happen at any time, and the victim is unable to distinguish the memory from actually experiencing the event again.
- Third, traumatized individuals often appear to be indifferent in order to mask the feelings of vulnerability and helplessness.[4]

Difficult as it may seem, it's important to recognize that these symptoms are normal reactions to abnormal circumstances. It may feel like you are out of control or going crazy, but what you are experiencing could well be post-traumatic stress.

For the average person, safety is the normal setting and anxiety is the occasional, unpleasant one. For those who have lived through trauma, fear and anxiety are the normal setting, while calmness and safety are rare to the point of being completely unfamiliar feelings.

Those with anxiety disorders may have an anxiety attack without consciously feeling anxious about anything. We may find ourselves terrified and afraid even when there is nothing threatening us. Because anxiety is our normal setting, it is there even when there is nothing to be anxious about. With this disorder, it isn't that we are anxious *about* something; rather, we are just anxious.

It doesn't help to tell an anxious person to stop worrying because, in fact, they aren't worrying—they are just experiencing their default setting.

―――――

In our family, trauma and the ensuing anxiety attacks are so common they are like the air we breathe, ever-present whether we are aware of them or not. Through the years, many well-meaning people have tried to fix us by quoting Bible verses, thinking an easy solution is at hand. One of the most often quoted passages is, "Do not be anxious about anything, but in every situation, by prayer and petition, with thanksgiving, present your requests to God. And the peace of God, which transcends all understanding, will guard your hearts and your minds in Christ Jesus" (Phil. 4:6–7).

Even though we know these folks mean well and truly want to help, for trauma victims who have endured the stigma and shame of mental illness and suffered acute panic attacks and anxiety disorders, these verses sound cheap. It seems like they are using the Bible to offer a spiritual Band-Aid rather than radical surgery and authentic healing. At the same time, deep down, we believe what the Bible is saying, so these verses stand. We know that God doesn't intend our lives to be marred by trauma, and his desire for us is peace and freedom.

The healing process, however, is often a long one. When there is shame, deep emotional wounds, fractured relationships, and unrelenting loneliness, trust doesn't come easily or quickly. When God seems to have disappointed us, prayer can be hard work. Where bitterness grips us, thanksgiving might appear shallow. As we experience healing, however, the potential of taking these verses as they stand will reappear. In the meantime, we must avoid the danger of cheap theology that clubs people into silence, as well as the danger of dismissing the Word whenever it doesn't seem to align with our current experience.

Your True Self

We've all been guilty of pretending to be people we're not. This might come from wanting to be accepted, fear, or simply a lack of self-awareness. The danger comes when we have worn a mask for so long we forget who we are underneath the surface.

Your true self is the most honest expression of who you are. It's the most authentic you, without all the masks, affectations, posturing, and pretensions, when you are most open, vulnerable, and comfortable in your own skin. Fred Rogers of *Mister Rogers' Neighborhood* reminded his young viewers, "The greatest gift you will ever give is your honest self."[5]

To be authentic doesn't mean we have to go on a search for our real self or try to become something we're not. It's about accepting ourselves without trying to make ourselves more genuine or real. It's about realizing and accepting the fact that we are flawed, and that is all right. This involves working with our strengths, accepting our weaknesses, and not trying to be anyone else.

To help get in touch with your true self, here are some things to try:

1. Work on self-awareness. Ask yourself who you are, what you like and dislike, what is important to you, and when you feel most comfortable.

2. Be honest and recognize who you are. Include positive and negative aspects; strengths and weaknesses; the weird, shameful parts; and the uncomfortable parts.

3. Stop pretending or imitating other people, which too often gets in the way of sincere efforts to express your real self.

4. Let emotions and feelings come to the surface and welcome vulnerability. Make a list of a variety of feelings and recognize how many you can get in touch with.

5. Don't look to others for validation. Realize that you will never be good enough for everyone, so don't waste your energy trying to please. Instead, focus on accepting all that you are.

6. Let go of fake and artificial relationships that don't support you expressing your true self. Letting go may give you a whole new sense of freedom.

Your False Self

People who have experienced trauma, particularly at a young age, may feel the need to protect themselves and their family by projecting a false self to the outside world. When feeling weak, inadequate, and damaged, it is common to develop a persona of strength, confidence, and sociability. This conceals the pain and brokenness, thus preserving an appearance of normality.

Usually the person expressing a persona is completely unaware of this dynamic and will argue to defend the false self the world sees. Like a stage actor putting on the mannerisms and expressions of their character, the person will adapt to perceived expectations and play the role they believe is expected of them. The whole world is a stage, and people are but the players on it, to paraphrase Shakespeare. This description applies to our efforts to present ourselves in a good light, even if we are playacting.

Perhaps sensing it isn't safe for them to be open about what is going on in their family, or inside themselves, they may learn to live a lie, because unconsciously they fear that if the truth comes out, it will overwhelm them and those they love.

The purpose of the false self is to hide and cope with unacknowledged pain. It takes courage to slowly peel away the layers of protective persona to reveal the real self that has been hidden. "When I get honest," writes Brennan Manning,

> I admit that I am a bundle of paradoxes. I believe and I doubt, I hope, and I get discouraged. I love and I hate; I feel bad about feeling good, I feel guilty about not feeling guilty. I am trusting and suspicious. I am honest and I still play games. Aristotle said I am a rational animal. I say I am an angel with an incredible capacity for beer.[6]

Trauma Can Lead to Further Health Problems

People who have experienced trauma in their lives may try to escape or cope by participating in risky behaviors such as drinking, smoking, using drugs, or overeating to comfort themselves.

Beyond unhealthy habits, though, our bodies also activate stress responses such as an increase in adrenaline levels, a racing heart, and a body that is primed to react. Chronic stress can increase inflammation in the body, which has been associated with a broad range of illnesses including cardiovascular and autoimmune diseases. Some children who experience trauma are more prone to health problems such as asthma, depression, stroke, and diabetes.

To complicate matters, people who have experienced trauma may also resist getting help. Avoidance is an important result of trauma. This is understandable, because if you experience something traumatic, you will want to avoid thinking about it or being reminded of it.

Our bodies react to stress in fairly predictable ways. Survival instincts kick in, increasing blood sugar for extra strength in our muscles and increased levels of cortisol to counter pain and inflammation. Increased endorphins can help us ignore physical pain.

All these physical reactions can result in bodily responses such as dizziness, nausea, shortness of breath, shaking, and sweating. There are also a number of psychological symptoms that can surface. These include intrusive thoughts, worry, difficulty sleeping, trouble focusing, bouts of crying, blame or self-judgment, as well as the inability to feel pleasure. The effects of trauma can also result in loneliness, anger, and general irritability.

Where Does Trauma Come From?

Physical or sexual abuse is clearly traumatic. One-time events like a car accident or a severe natural disaster can be traumatizing as well.

Ongoing stress, such as living in a dangerous neighborhood or being the victim of bullying, can also be traumatic, especially for a child. Nearly any event could be seen as traumatic to a child if it happened unexpectedly or repeatedly. If someone was intentionally cruel in the child's eyes, trauma occurs, as well as when destructive things happen that the child was unprepared for, intentional or not. The traumatic event doesn't even have to happen directly to the child. Watching someone else suffering can also be a source of trauma.

Not everyone who endures a tragedy or a near-death experience will necessarily have trauma. Some will be less affected by their experiences than others.

Troubling Symptoms of Trauma

Following a traumatic event, there can be dozens of symptoms and problems welling up inside the person.

Hearing Voices

One of the most upsetting and baffling experiences for trauma victims can be the intrusive and seemingly unstoppable hearing of voices. Often, these voices maintain a low, constant background drone, interrupted by startling screams of abusive epithets that can be mocking, demeaning, and horrific. As they continue unabated, the trauma victim can come to see themselves as completely worthless, shameful, or even demon-possessed. Thoughts of suicide can also torment the person.

It's not unusual for this painful distraction to be occurring while the person is attempting to appear normal in their daily routine. Other people usually don't recognize there is a debilitating undercurrent just below the surface that is distracting and undermining the trauma victim as they strive to appear normal.

CNN news announcer Anderson Cooper did a segment on his program in which he wore earphones that simulated the experience of intrusive thoughts and auditory hallucinations. He tried to function normally, which included taking brief tests, making conversation, and walking down the street in New York. Finally, after failing the tests, realizing that he couldn't carry on conversationally, and being overwhelmed with frustration, he ended the segment.[7]

The audience can hear the voices he is hearing. It is both eerie and disturbing. My friends who suffer from intrusive thoughts have told me this was the first time they had seen their inner experience presented in a real, honest, and meaningful way.

Memories, Nightmares, and Flashbacks

Other symptoms of trauma include three experiences that appear similar but have important distinctions: memories, nightmares, and flashbacks.

Replaying *memories* are frequently described by trauma survivors. They find that their mind keeps replaying the painful memory almost endlessly. This is particularly disturbing, because getting it out of their mind is often a primary goal. Perhaps the mind is trying to make some sense of the experience, or maybe it's processing, searching for different responses that could have helped at the time. Whatever the reason behind the looping memories, it is frustrating to not be able to turn them off or make them stop.

Similarly, *nightmares* frequently haunt our dreams after a trauma experience. Nightmares may not reenact the event, nor are they always about the event, although common themes surface, like danger, dread, foreboding, paralysis, and fleeing. They will often cause us to experience poor sleep, and in some cases, the fear of having the nightmares causes people to try to avoid sleeping at all, which creates even more problems.

Flashbacks happen when the trauma experience suddenly seems like it is happening to us again. This can occur when we are awake, asleep, or even in the time between sleeping and awakening. Actual physical reactions such as lashing out or falling down, terror, shouting, and fleeing can accompany flashbacks.

I asked my son, who is a trauma survivor, what the difference between memories and flashbacks was for him. He described memories as looking at postcards from a past vacation, while flashbacks were actually reliving the experience. Flashbacks are like an alarm set off in the brain, releasing a torrent of emotions and vivid flashes of the trauma.

Usually traumatic memories and flashbacks are awakened by triggers, which remind the person of the past traumatic experience. Sounds, sights, even smells can alert the mind and cause a post-traumatic reaction. Often, seemingly insignificant events in our lives serve as triggers. Disruptions to our daily routine, anniversaries, loneliness, feelings of rejection, perceived threats, or feeling out of control can trigger a trauma response.

Many trauma survivors describe a sense of being disconnected from their environment and even from themselves. It's as if they are living in two worlds at the same time: the trauma world and the physical world. Though they try to live in the "real world," their memories, nightmares, and flashbacks keep pulling them back to the trauma world.

———

When a terrible thing happens to us, no matter our age, it is natural to think it happened because we are a terrible person. In that way, it becomes part of our identity. Not only do we reason that bad things happen because we are bad but also we believe that other people can't care for us—because the very people we looked to for care did not take care of us. Psychologist Bessel van der Kolk observes, "It's really about having difficulty feeling alive in the present, feeling engaged, feeling a sense of pleasure, of joy, of even exuberance at the right moment, of just feeling like it's good to be alive."[8]

A big part of understanding trauma is realizing that the brain doesn't distinguish between physical threats and emotional threats. The response in our bodies is the same. This is why so many physical symptoms are connected to past trauma. Rapid heartbeat, increased adrenaline, higher blood pressure, sweating, physical tics, uncontrolled gestures—all are ways your body is telling you to *get out now*!

It isn't unusual to want to hold back what you're feeling and deny or attempt to bury the upsetting feelings. Instead, talk about your thoughts, feelings, and reactions to the events with people you trust. Then, talk about your trauma some more. Keep talking about it until you have no need to talk about it anymore.

Do whatever it takes to create a safe environment for yourself. Set up your surroundings in a way that makes you feel safe and comfortable. You may need to leave a light on when you sleep, play soothing music, or interact with a pet. Recognize that recovery takes time, and you are in a process that is quite different from an instant cure. If you had the flu, you'd need to follow the necessary steps to fully recover and move forward in a healthy way, right? Give yourself the same freedom as you recover from traumatic stress.

Take positive action on your own behalf. If you were sexually abused as a child, report it to child protective services. If you were a victim of crime, consider prosecuting the person who did this to you. It can be an empowering experience to report the crime to authorities and press charges if possible. Sometimes this isn't an option for you, but you can still be proactive by writing in a journal, using words to stand up to the abuser. And through it all, professional help from a therapist or trauma counselor can make a great difference in aiding your recovery.

Be patient with yourself. Healing takes time, and you will go through ups and downs. Remind yourself that what happened wasn't okay, but you are okay now, and you will be okay in the future.

9

It Takes Ten "Atta-Boys" to Make Up for Every "You Jerk"

Any fool can criticize, condemn and complain—and most fools do.
— Dale Carnegie

One of the biggest files in my office was the one in which I kept all the hate mail I'd received over the years. Pastors I talk with agree that the amount of angry, bitter, and just plain mean letters we receive, which often include personal attacks and critiques of our families as well, far outweighs the loving, kind, affirming, and appreciative notes. Whether there is actually more hate mail than love letters, we don't know. But it seems like there are many more, simply because of the negative impact these notes of "constructive criticism" wreak on our hearts and minds.

One afternoon, my friend Bruce asked me where I kept all the positive letters I'd received. I confessed that after I read them, I'd throw them away. Then I told him of my giant archive file of negative mail. He was shocked. Not shocked that I had negative letters; he knew everyone gets those. But shocked that I kept them and threw away the positive notes. "Are you crazy?" He laughed. "Take all those files of mean letters and throw them away right now. Then start a new file where you can save all the affirming thank-you cards and notes of appreciation." I guess I had been doing it all wrong.

Negative Sticks

Negative memories are remembered more than positive ones. In general, we tend to notice the negative more than the positive. Laura Carstensen, a psychology professor at Stanford University, points out that this may have occurred throughout history. "It's more important for people, for survival, to notice the lion in the brush than it is to notice the beautiful flower that's growing on the other side of the way."[1]

That sounds right to me. When I was a kid growing up in West Africa, we were constantly on the alert for potential danger from animals, snakes, giant insects, and other humans. If something went wrong in the jungle where we lived, it could turn out very badly. Survival demanded focusing more on the negatives than the positives. Of course, returning home to Southern California didn't stop me from focusing primarily on negative things. I suppose I brought negativity back with me.

However, it's not just me. An inclination to focus on the negative shows itself in different ways. We have a tendency to remember bad things more readily and in greater detail than good things. We describe negative things more vividly and with stronger language than we do positive things. We also assume a person making negative comments is smarter than someone who speaks positively. Criticism tends to have more impact and influence and stays with us longer than praise. It is the go-to approach for performance evaluations at work, and it is often glazed over with a soft covering of "helpful criticism."

The TV show *The Simpsons* even illustrated the power of criticism in the episode where Homer Simpson is the only person to criticize filmmaker Mel Gibson's new movie. "Oh, Mel," says Homer, "it's the most boring piece of garbage I've ever seen, and it's not easy for me to say that."[2] Mel assumes this criticism from Homer must indicate that Homer is smarter than anyone else, so he enlists him to help make his movie. Spoiler alert: it doesn't turn out well.

Our memories are also in a state of constant flux, because our brains will reshape a memory every time we recall it. And each time we retell a memory, we become more confident of its accuracy, because we have told and retold it so many times. Carstensen says, "Memories are fallible. Long-term memories are nearly always wrong."[3]

Criticisms have a greater impact than praise or compliments, and bad news often draws more attention than good. The reason is that negative events have a greater impact on our brains than positive ones. This is what psychologists refer to as a *negative bias*. This bias is our tendency to pay more attention to criticism than to praise. It means we will feel the pain of putdowns more powerfully than we will feel the pleasure of praise.

One of my favorite comedy writers and actors is Kevin Hart. He started out in standup comedy clubs, like most comedians, before he found success and became rich and famous as a hysterically funny comedian. He relates a story that shows the power of negative feedback.

> Lucien Hold was a legend. . . . Every great comedian from Chris Rock to Jerry Seinfeld had gone through this same audition with him. . . . Fortunately, I had an unbelievable set that night. I was on fire, the audience exploded, the room was destroyed. . . . Afterward, Lucien called me into the back room. I joined him, excited to get feedback from the legend himself.
>
> He sat me down, adjusted his shirt, and spoke: "I don't think this is for you. . . . I didn't get it. The jokes didn't resonate for me." I stared at him dumbfounded. "I've been watching comedy for some time. I've seen the best of the best. I've seen them all, and I don't see it in you."
>
> I stuttered something incomprehensible. How could it be that the audience was laughing so much, if I wasn't any good?
>
> "I'm just being honest and straight up rather than holding things back," he continued. "I don't want you to waste your time. . . . "
>
> At that moment, I felt my heart drop out of my chest. . . . His words cut deeper than any insult I'd experienced before. If he'd been racist, at least I could have understood where the hate was coming from. But this was specifically about my talent, or lack thereof. My whole comedy life passed before my eyes.[4]

Even now, after achieving a brilliant comedy career in which he earns millions of dollars a year, it's intriguing that Kevin remembers in such detail the pain of that one negative critique. I also think if Lucien the Legend were asked now, looking back, if he was wrong in his destructive criticism of Kevin Hart, he'd probably stand his ground and refuse to budge in his opinion.

Sadly, most of us have had run-ins with a "Lucien" in this world. Hopefully, they have not been able to derail us or destroy our dreams. But the pain is real, and the damage they do to our confidence is long-lasting. For these reasons, it is important to understand how negative criticism affects us and what we can do to overcome it.

It is the negative things that grab our attention, stick in our memories, and even influence our decision-making. Nobel Prize–winning researchers Daniel Kahneman and Amos Tversky found that when making decisions, people consistently place greater weight on negative aspects of an event than they do on positive ones.[5]

This tendency to overemphasize the negative can have an impact on the choices we make and risks we are willing to take. For example, when thinking about a scenario involving gaining an amount of money or losing the same amount of money, the risk of loss tends to loom larger in people's minds. People have a stronger negative reaction to losing $20 than the positive feelings they have from gaining $20.[6]

One day while playing golf with my friend Dave, I suddenly became particularly competitive and intensely focused toward the very end of our match. He told me it seemed like I really wanted to win. I thought for a minute then let him know that I didn't care at all about winning but I hated the thought of losing, especially to him! Perhaps this is because while winning feels good for a little bit, losing feels bad for a lot longer.

———

Since we naturally give more weight to negative things, how do we begin to change our way of thinking and fight this tendency toward a negative bias? The answer is not flipping over to a positive bias, because that would be no healthier. The goal is to recognize our bias, begin to balance our perspectives, and gain a healthy equilibrium in our thinking that includes equal parts negative and positive input.

If you find yourself mulling over and mentally chewing on a negative experience or memory, don't just sit there; get up and change your focus just like you'd change the channel on the TV. Call a friend, play some music, take the dog for a walk, do anything to break your mood and end the ruminating.

Because it takes more for positive experiences to be remembered, we need to give extra attention to good things that happen to us and positive things that people say to us. Resist the natural urge to dismiss or minimize a positive and take some time to recall it and replay the moment several times in your mind, focusing on the good feelings you experienced at that moment. It is easy to tell a friend about a bad experience or some put-down you endured from a coworker, so it's all the more important to tell someone about a good thing that happened.

With nothing to do, the mind is unable to prevent negative thoughts from elbowing their way to center stage. Worries about one's love life, health, investments, family, and job are always hovering at the periphery of attention, waiting until there is nothing pressing that demands concentration. As soon as the mind is ready to relax, zap! The potential problems that were waiting in the wings take over.[7]

Signs of a Negative Bias

The bias toward negativity shows itself in many ways as we go through our day-to-day experiences.

- We remember insults more than we remember praise.
- Negative experiences tend to be more memorable than positive ones.
- Our brains tend to be wary and vigilant, always on guard for possible threats.
- For positive experiences to resonate, they must occur much more frequently than negative ones.
- The brain reacts more strongly to negative stimuli than to positive stimuli.
- If something good and something bad happen to us on the same day, we'll react more strongly to the bad than to the good.
- When the mind wanders, it's more likely to recall something that made us angry or upset, instead of recalling something that made us happy and filled us with pride.

Left unchecked, a negative bias can be a serious impediment to our happiness and quality of life. But as we learn to deal with it, we can immediately start improving our quality of life.

The first step is recognizing that a problem exists. Knowing that we have a negative bias helps us realize when we are dwelling on the negative aspects of a situation because of it. If you find that is what is happening, you can remind yourself that this bias is all it is.

Neuropsychologist Rick Hanson says, "Our brains are like Velcro for negative experiences and like Teflon for positive ones."[8] That being the case, it makes sense that negative things get stored quickly in our memory while positive experiences need to be held in our thoughts for a longer time period. This bit of extra attention to the positive thing allows time to transfer it from our short-term memory to our long-term memory.

Hanson recommends, when something positive happens to us, to make it a point to take a moment to savor the positive experience. We should replay it in our minds a few times so that it gets stored in our long-term memory. He adds that "you absorb the positive experience like gentle rain falling on your skin."[9]

I believe it takes ten "atta-boys" to make up for one "you jerk." Now, I may be overstating the number a little, but the concept is still true. Because of the negative bias, it is important to realize other people will be much more affected by the negative things we say or do than the positive ones. This means if you scold a child, criticize a coworker, or argue with your spouse, you'd better be prepared to say and do a whole lot of positive things just to maintain a healthy relationship with them. If we mistakenly think that maintaining a 50-50 balance of criticisms and compliments will make everything all right, then, like my mother often told me, "You've got another think coming!"

The Power of Praise

"I have yet to find the man, however exalted his station," said Charles Schwab, "who did not do better work and put forth greater effort under a spirit of approval than under a spirit of criticism."[10] When we praise someone, it can be a powerful and effective way of bringing out the best in the person.

Proverbs compares praise to the refining process of silver and gold. The refining fire and intense heat separate impurities, resulting in purity. "The crucible is for silver and the furnace for gold, and each is tested by the praise accorded him" (Prov. 27:21 NASB). In the same way that the conventional refining process brings out the purity of the metals, through praise the best qualities of a person can become visible, strengthened, and developed. This purifying occurs for both the one who is praised and the one who praises.

Psalm 22:3 reminds us that God inhabits the praises of his people. God's presence, love, and power are alive as we offer praise to him. The flip side of this verse also has clear implications: God does not live where we mutter, criticize, and complain.

The Gospel of John describes a dinner party where Mary of Bethany took a pint of pure nard, an expensive perfume, and poured it on Jesus's feet, then wiped them with her hair as the fragrance of the expensive perfume filled the entire house.

Of course, as is too often the case, she was criticized and shamed for her extravagant gesture. On the surface, the criticism seemed to make sense, combining a perfect blend of concern for the poor, hypocrisy, and fiscal responsibility. Like a lot of our criticisms, it had a certain logic that most folks might have agreed with. But Jesus would have none of it. "Leave her alone!" he demanded (see John 12:1–8).

When we praise someone with truthful compliments and affirmations, we bring out positive characteristics that help us be better people. Like Jesus, we can also stop hurtful criticisms by shutting up the bullies with their demeaning comments and shallow critiques.

There is a big difference between honest praise and flattery. On the surface they can seem similar, but in reality they are complete opposites. Flattery is insincere and often manipulative. When we use flattery, it's often to butter someone up in order to get something from them. Praise tends to be more natural and expresses delight in the things we value about the other person.

It's easy to feel trapped after receiving flattery, because it often is a trap. "Those who flatter their neighbors are spreading nets for their feet" (Prov. 29:5). If we thought we'd received an honest compliment but then realized it was part of a manipulation, it can be hard not to feel resentful. Sometimes we hold back on compliments because we don't want people to think we are using flattery. Likewise, when we are given an honest compliment it can be difficult to receive because we wonder if it is simply shallow flattery.

"You know we never used flattery," the apostle Paul writes, "nor did we put on a mask to cover up greed—God is our witness. We were not looking for praise from people, not from you or anyone else. . . . Because we loved you so much, we were delighted to share with you not only the gospel of God but our lives as well" (1 Thess. 2:5–6, 8).

Something else that can help us when we find ourselves getting out of balance and leaning toward our negative bias is to schedule lots of small and simple positive experiences throughout the day. Too often we try to hold out for big events, like a vacation, a party, or a special large purchase, but these big things are too infrequent to effectively counter the bias.

Rather than wait for something big to occur, seek out small positive experiences, which can be things like taking time to read a few pages of a book you enjoy, playing music, enjoying a good cup of coffee when you aren't rushing somewhere, and showing kindness to someone. These little bits of positivity throughout the day will help the brain counteract its natural negativity.

Sometimes showing a person respect or an act of kindness can be more powerful than overt praise. Tony Campolo, while speaking at a church I pastored in Minnesota, shared about a shopping trip to Nordstrom that he took with his wife to help her look for a new outfit. When they arrived at the store, he did what most husbands do when their wives are shopping at Nordstrom: he sat in a chair and pretended to listen to the piano player. He couldn't help but notice a woman who appeared to be a bag lady from the street. She was older, unkempt, and carried a bunch of stuff with her.

She walked around the women's clothes department, looking at displays and racks of clothing, then called out to one of the sales associates, "How much is this dress?"

The sales associate said, "It's $1,200."

"Okay, I want to try it on," the woman replied.

"Before you do," the worker said, "here are some things that might go well with the dress. Why don't you try them all on and see how you like them?"

After a while the lady came out of the dressing room and handed back all the clothes. "No, I don't like any of them," the lady said. "I'm not going to buy anything today."

She then turned and started walking away. The sales associate said, "Wait a minute!" The woman stopped and looked down at the floor. "The next time you come in here to try on clothes, here is my business card," the worker said, handing a card to her. "I want you to ask for me. It would be an honor to serve you."[11]

Having lived in Seattle, I'm accustomed to hearing stories about the extraordinary service that Nordstrom is known for. But this account reminded me that a simple act of treating people with dignity, not judging on appearance, and showing respect may be the most powerful gifts we could give to someone.

What We Need to Know to Live Like There's No Yesterday

The whole Bible in six words: God loves you—don't be stupid. — Bruce Larson

I used to think the Bible was complicated and hard to understand. It was easy for me to get bogged down while trying to read it; after all, it seemed foreign and unconnected to the issues I was dealing with. At the same time, I wanted to grasp what it said and apply its lessons to my life, and I wanted to get to the core truth of Scripture if that was at all possible.

When we overcomplicate things, it gives us an excuse so we don't have to deal with them. Some folks avoid applying the message of the Bible personally because they think it's too complicated. As if we had to understand electrical engineering and be able to dismantle and rebuild our TV before watching it! If that were true, I'd never watch any shows. Or as my dad, who was mechanically inclined, told me, I shouldn't get my driver's license until I could take apart a car engine and rebuild it. Of course, if I'd listened I'd still be waiting for the bus.

So, when my friend Bruce mentioned that he had figured out the message of the whole Bible and it consisted of only six words, I was a bit skeptical. But when he told me, "God loves you—don't be stupid," I knew he was right. If we're going to live like there's no yesterday, we can't do better than beginning there.

Some of us struggle to grasp the message "God loves you," and others have difficulty coming to terms with "don't be stupid." It's important to hear both sides of the message. If we miss God's love and focus only on "don't be stupid," we may go our whole lives trying not to make mistakes and totally miss the compassionate care God intends for us. Likewise, feeling only "love," we might end up hurting ourselves and others because we do so many stupid things.

When it comes to love, I think most people believe it is important. No one has to convince us that it would be great to be more loving or to have others love us more. Who wouldn't want that? In fact, it's such a no-brainer, it might be one of the few things we can all agree about, which should indicate it isn't an issue for us. Except for one little thing: it doesn't always work out the way we want. While we might all agree love is important, love doesn't grow without our coming to grips with the second truth: don't be stupid.

We Are All Stupid

We've all done stupid stuff. Even really smart people lose their mind and do stupid things. The Darwin Awards, for instance, have gained a cult following for recognizing people who've died in the most compellingly stupid ways. While I don't believe many of us intentionally set out to be stupid, the frequency of the behavior makes me wonder why a normal, intelligent person would put themselves in harm's way for so little good reason. For example, in 2008 a Catholic priest named Father Adelir Antonio attempted a stunt to publicize his plans to build a spiritual rest stop for truckers. He got the idea from "Lawn Chair Larry," who had attached forty-five weather balloons to his lawn chair and took off flying over Los Angeles.

Because Larry survived, the priest thought he would too. And he actually took a lot of commonsense precautions, such as sitting in a buoyant chair, wearing a survival suit and parachute, packing a satellite phone, and also bringing a GPS device. What could possibly go wrong?

There was one problem with his plan. After he took off, the winds shifted, pushing him out over the ocean. At that point he could've jumped and used his parachute for a safe landing, but he figured since he had his satellite phone and GPS, he would be smart and keep on flying in his chair.

After a while, drifting farther and farther out to sea, he used his satellite phone to call for help. The only problem was that the Coast Guard couldn't locate him—because he didn't know how to use the GPS he carried with him. As he struggled with the device over the course of several hours, and those on the phone with him struggled to explain how it should work, his phone finally died and he disappeared forever.[1]

People who may be very intelligent and educated about certain things are also capable of doing incredibly stupid things. This problem is intensified if people are obviously being stupid but are unable to see the problem and actually defend themselves as being clever. Cornell University psychologists have studied how people fail to recognize their errors. They showed that when people do stupid things they suffer from a dual burden: first, they are dim-witted, and second, they lack the cognitive ability to recognize this.[2]

They began this study because of a monumentally stupid crook, McArthur Wheeler, who robbed two banks in Pittsburgh without wearing a mask. Security camera video of the robberies clearly showing the face of the criminal was played on local telecasts. Within minutes, tips as to his identity reached police, and before the day was done Wheeler was in custody. He couldn't believe his bad luck and told detectives, "But I wore the juice." It seems Wheeler had found out that lemon juice can be used as invisible ink. So, he reasoned, if he put lemon juice on his face he would be invisible to security cameras.[3]

This isn't a recent phenomenon; people have been stupid for a long time. The Bible tells us that when God created the world, at every stage of creation he pronounced it good. Even when he made humankind, he said it was good. Actually, he said man was good and woman was very good. All of life was meant to be good. God was good, the world was good, and people were good.

There was only one thing that would wreck everything, and God was very clear that he didn't want people to know or experience evil. So they were forbidden from partaking of the fruit of the tree of the knowledge of good and evil. Wouldn't it be enough to just know and enjoy the good? But that evidently wasn't enough, because Adam and Eve wanted to know what God knew; they wanted to know and experience evil. Up until then, stupid didn't exist. But by Adam and Eve demanding the right to know evil, stupidity entered the world. Perhaps Oscar

Wilde recognized this when he said, "There is no sin except stupidity."[4]

Lest you think that stupidity is only reserved for the few, we are all stupid from time to time. Stupidity isn't only for some of us; it's a universal human trait. The good news is that even when we are stupid, God still loves us.

We Are All Loved

In order to experience the true freedom that comes from living like there's no yesterday, we need to embrace both sides of the message. It isn't enough to experience God's unconditional love if we continue to behave stupidly. And stopping stupid behavior without knowing we are loved can leave us rigid, lonely, and judgmental.

What are some of the things that make it difficult for us to receive the love we long for and to demonstrate love to others, even those we care about the most? Some of it has to do with choices. All of us have choices to make, which can sometimes make us feel powerful because we can decide between options that affect our lives. In a way we are powerful, because we have the ability to block our experience of being loved. The Bible makes it quite clear that we are loved by God regardless. Whether we deserve it or not, whether we are responsive or not, God loves us unconditionally. Despite this, many of us go through life not able to accept or receive God's love for us.

A while back, I was in Phoenix being interviewed for a program that was to be broadcast in Canada. Seemingly out of the blue, the host asked what I thought was one of our biggest fears. Without thinking, I blurted out, "It's the fear of being found out." When the host looked at me with that "What are you talking about?" gaze, I realized that I'd simply let slip one of my own biggest fears, without regard to anyone else. But after a commercial break, we were able to talk about how afraid we all were of being found out.

Maybe it's one of our least acknowledged fears, and we all need to address it. Because we do all fear being found out. Maybe we fear people will discover we aren't the person we try to present ourselves as being. Nor are we the person we wish we were, or that others think we are. In my case, I had to admit that I was afraid people might discover I wasn't what they expected as a pastor or an author who wrote about life and faith with insight, compassion, and tenderness that obviously came from my devout lifestyle and loving, trouble-free relationships, combined with a relaxed sense of humor and the innate ability to always respond appropriately in any given situation.

What if my cover was blown? What if people discovered that, in fact, I was (and am) just a guy trying to figure stuff out? Sometimes I make a mess of things, and much of the time I'm just trying to discover how to live and follow Jesus without hurting too many people along the way. If people found out that I'm no different from them, they probably wouldn't want me to be their pastor—or even their friend.

The need to protect ourselves by preserving an image of how we want others to see us didn't start with us. In the garden of Eden, right after being stupid, Adam and Eve hid themselves because they were afraid of being found out. And we've been hiding ever since, not wanting our stupidity to be revealed. This choice to protect ourselves can prevent us from experiencing God's love.

In spite of this, we are loved regardless, though sometimes it is difficult to accept love or feel God's love for us. We often carry lots of positive expectations about what it means to be loved, what love is or isn't, what love should be or could be, and how we ought to be treated. We also have a few negative expectations, maybe even thoughts like, *I got hurt once, so I'm not going to let anyone get close to me again. They'll probably just hurt me like before.* If we are expecting something negative to happen, it's understandable why we don't want to go there.

The trouble begins when we have unrealistic ideas about how things ought to be. Perhaps we glean ideas from others, or our expectations for love get shaped by movies, books, and songs, until we end up with illusion and fantasy instead of real love in our real lives. It's too easy to compare a fantasy ideal with our down-to-earth relationships and get tempted to pursue the fantasy. Before long, we can lose perspective of what real love is.

The Temptation to Keep God at a Distance

It is impossible to experience God's love while maintaining an attitude of fear. Either fear will block the love, or love will take away the fear. Love and fear cannot coexist inside us. We are reminded in the Bible that "perfect love casts out fear" (1 John 4:18 ESV), while our fearfulness tries to block our experience of love. It keeps us from getting involved in life, it holds us back from engaging with other people, it stops us from involvement in our world, and it certainly leads us to hold back from engaging with God.

In counseling, I've met many people who are hesitant about relating to God. It often comes down to thinking God is mean, angry, distant, or aloof. So they don't want to get too close. It's better to maintain a nice, comfortable, respectful distance than to let God love them. Because if they allow the Lord to get too close, they might get hurt.

Where does our perception of God come from? I think our view of God is formed in large part by how we viewed and related to our earthly fathers when we were about ten years old. If your dad was loving and involved in your life, it is easier and more natural to hear that your heavenly Father loves you and to accept it without hesitation. But what if your dad was angry and abusive? It would be understandable to pull away from a God who is seen to be punishing and hurtful.

Perhaps your father was more of an absentee landlord who was distant and aloof, who didn't engage or take a personal interest in his children but every once in a while seemed to swoop in and enforce rules—that you might not have even been aware of—before going away again, leaving turmoil and distress in his wake. Is it any wonder you might grow up feeling that God is distant and punitive?

My father-in-law was a Marine who believed in strict discipline for the children. Although my wife, Eileen, worked hard to never make a mistake, she has admitted that it wasn't until many years later that she began to understand God loved her.

I, on the other hand, fought against my dad and everybody else, challenging authority wherever I was confronted by it. It was a breakthrough for me when a pastor I respected told me that God wasn't like my dad. He let me know that I was free to fight against what I considered irrational authority while at the same time living in a relationship with Christ, whose authority I didn't need to challenge because it was grounded in love.

Whatever our relationship with our earthly dads, it doesn't have to define or limit our relationship with God today. We are free to live beyond those formative attitudes and experiences, whether they were positive or negative. We are free to let God love us.

The Danger of Drifting

Sometimes when we get busy in life, we have commitments, frustrations, cares, and responsibilities that can overwhelm us. We feel the need to take care of our family or our business, or just live life without dealing with God's love or the implications of loving others on a daily basis. I understand that sometimes it can all feel a bit overwhelming, and we might want to control the things we assume are controllable and let everything else slide. It is very easy to just drift.

While visiting my family in San Diego, I was chatting with my brother Richard and his wife, Donna. It wasn't long before the conversation turned to our grown kids. When I asked how things were going with their sons, Thomas and David, my sister-in-law smiled brightly and shared how David had really found himself and had become a drifter. That seemed odd to me, but I smiled stupidly and mumbled something about what good news it was to hear. She nodded warmly and said, "Yes, we are all so proud of him."

Did I hear this correctly? It sounded a little wacky, even for our family. And yet it appeared like they didn't see a problem with their son being a drifter. I was starting to feel sorry for them as I pictured my nephew all alone drifting from town to town, carrying his meager possessions in a sack thrown over his shoulder, like the hobos of a previous era, and lining up at the food bank or homeless shelter.

"What's wrong with you people?" I wanted to shout. Then I was about to suggest how we might all pitch in to help him get back on his feet. But before I could share my plan, my brother got out his phone and began showing me pictures of David's drifting. That's when I learned drifting was actually what they called a special form of underground car racing in which the racers spin and slide at high speeds in their special cars. Evidently, my nephew was quite good at drifting in his red Ferrari. Wow, was I out of touch!

Drifting is only mentioned one time in the Bible, in the admonition to not "drift away" in Hebrews 2:1. I doubt it refers to underground car racing, but there are a couple of ways we might drift away. One image of drifting is by the process of evaporation, which occurs when we boil water. Heat causes the water to turn to steam, which rises (drifts away) until all the water is gone and the pan is left on the stove to burn. Anyone who survived a junior high science lab can tell us this form of drifting is the change from one substance (water) to a less substantial substance (steam).

This reminds me of the original *Back to the Future* movie, when Michael J. Fox's character, Marty McFly, is playing guitar at the school dance. Glancing down, he sees first his hand then his arm beginning to disappear as he is changing into a person of less substance. He is starting to drift.

We can also drift away when we become distracted and allow ourselves to be diverted from our intentions and goals. Momentum can help us reach our goals or it can hurt us by carrying us in unhealthy directions. When the Bible cautions us to not drift away, it is a warning to not be stupid and allow momentum to carry us into danger. We might not intend to drift into trouble, but we find ourselves losing control and hurting ourselves and those around us.

I learned about the potentially destructive power of momentum once when I was messing around with friends and did something incredibly stupid. While living in California, I was part of a small group of guys who met early every Wednesday morning in my office, where we'd study the Bible, share personally, and try to encourage each other as a group.

We decided to go on an outing together, so we took a trip to the region known as "gold country," where we spent the day jet skiing on a lake. It was a fun day together—almost. I wasn't very experienced in driving jet skis, but I was soon able to ride around like the others and navigate the lake in a fairly confident way.

After several hours of riding around the lake, I sensed the mood slightly change as some of my friends began to pick on me. As I'd be riding along, one would come by and accelerate his jet ski while turning slightly, which sent a wave of water crashing over me, knocking me off my jet ski, while the others laughed at me bobbing in the lake.

This little game continued on into the afternoon, and my frustration kept growing. Though I smiled and laughed along with the others, it brought up some memories of childhood bullies who'd thought it was fun to mess with me. Of course I hated it.

Then I got focused. It was payback time! We were near the end of the day and had decided to take one more zip around the lake before heading home. I kept my eyes on Dave (who had dumped me in the lake more than anyone else). It was time to teach him a lesson he would never forget.

I saw him sitting quietly on his jet ski, getting ready to get off the water, and I headed straight at him, picking up speed as I accelerated in his direction. I aimed my jet ski right at him, going faster and faster, and I noticed a flicker of confusion in his eyes as if he wondered what I was doing. The others had grown silent as they watched me bear down on him. Then just when it seemed I was going to crash into him at full speed, I turned, intending to send a big wall of water crashing down on him. Laughing victoriously at my brilliant act of revenge, I turned around to celebrate my perfect payback.

Why was everyone yelling at me as if I had done something wrong?

Evidently, there is a principle in physics that indicates an object in motion will continue in motion. Not being a physicist, it hadn't occurred to me that when I turned away from Dave so that he would be splashed by water, the back half of my jet ski would continue to move forward at high speed. I had ridden up over Dave's jet ski with such force I sheared off the steering column and control handles.

The others told me how, in a desperate attempt to save his life, Dave had leapt into the air, hurling himself away from the collision like a Hollywood stuntman, narrowly missing being cut in half or decapitated by my jet ski.

I puttered slowly over to where he was floating quietly in the water and asked if he was all right. He nodded yes but looked like he was concentrating on something important. I asked him what he was doing and he responded, "I'm counting my fingers and toes to see if they are all still attached." That day I learned an important lesson: momentum is not helpful when we are doing something incredibly stupid.

Love Is

With these attitudes and choices at work, is it any wonder we struggle to understand what love actually is? Love is not just a warm feeling or some big abstract concept. Some people have such a grand ideal of love that they never get around to expressing it in the simple kindness of ordinary life. They may even dream of idealized love expressed in heroic devotion and sacrificing service. But while waiting for the opportunity that never comes, they make themselves irritating and quite unlikable for those near them, and may never tune in to their neighbor's need. It's easy to get caught up in a marvelous concept of love and miss the tangible expression of it in our everyday lives.

In spite of our defenses or choices that keep us from knowing we are loved regardless of anything we have done or not done, God loves us. Nothing changes that fact. And while love can be expressed in a variety of ways and in all kinds of different settings, there are some common traits to help us identify it in our lives.

First, love *moves toward*. Rather than settling into a comfort zone, love compels us to move toward. It doesn't pull away, hide, or become passive. Love involves engaging in all types of circumstances and finding ways to come alongside, listen, and act with compassion. This is true whether we are seeking to love our neighbor, ourselves, or God. There is no hiding or withdrawing in a loving relationship. God, in love, moves toward us, and we in turn step out of our comfort zone to care for the world around us.

This can go against many of our natural tendencies and habits of holding back, pushing away, walling off, and keeping control. When we choose to move toward another person, it is essentially a choice to lose control. And that is a risk worth taking.

Second, love *isn't safe*. I wish this weren't true, I really do. I wish I could only be in relationships that are safe, free from misunderstandings, failure, disappointment, grief, and brokenness. In my idealized world, that would be so great.

But then I realize if my relationships were safe like that, I'd be so bored.

Safety and security are not traits of authentic love. C. S. Lewis points this out in his Chronicles of Narnia series. In *The Lion, the Witch and the Wardrobe*, when the children first hear of Aslan the lion, little Lucy asks, "Then he isn't safe?" "'Course he isn't safe," Mr. Beaver replies. "But he is good."[5]

Our desire to feel safe and secure can keep us from experiencing God's goodness. But instead of drawing inward, real love propels us out on an adventure.

Third, love *avoids bartering*. So many times our relationships fall into the bog of tradeoffs. "What would you give me if I did this or stopped doing that?" There is no freedom when love is reduced to negotiation. Freedom is experienced when we realize we are loved regardless. Then we can be ourselves, we can share and care with abandon, and we can relate to others with openness and vulnerability.

I've been fortunate to have friendships with an amazing variety of people through the years. For example, I met Gary when we were both young pastors in very different settings. I was on the West Coast, and he was in central Illinois. I liked the sound of the ocean, and he preferred the sound of wind blowing through the cornfields. I was in a large mainline church, and he was in a church that probably wouldn't have considered me a real Christian. But we became friends and basically walked through our lives together.

We'd meet up now and then and spend several days talking about our lives, the good and the bad and the ugly. Through the years, we both went through struggles, successes, failures, joys, and sorrows. We could share deeply because we didn't need to hide, maintain an image, or impress one another. We weren't impressed or disappointed in each other, nor did we offer much advice or instruction. We were just two guys sharing our lives. His friendship over the years showed me what it means to be loved regardless, and it made me want to develop other friendships like ours in which there wasn't pressure to act a certain way or try to fix each other, because we became better people just by being loved without conditions.

Going Deeper

A lot of the wanting that goes on in the world—wanting our way, wanting everything for ourselves, wanting to appear important—has nothing to do with what God wants for us; it just isolates us from him. It's like we put up walls of what we want, and in so doing we keep God out of our lives.

Maybe it's just easier to focus on the things of the world even though we already know they won't result in freedom or joy. When the Bible tells us, "Do not love the world or the things in the world" (1 John 2:15 ESV), it may be for a very good reason. Our tendency is to love things and use people, which is exactly opposite of what we are supposed to do. We are supposed to love people and use things!

Part of realizing that God loves us is rooted in understanding that he made us. We are his creation, his children, and the object of his love. It's mind-boggling to consider that our lives, each different and unique, with abilities and shortcomings, hopes and fears, idiosyncrasies, fascinating experiences, and embarrassing failures, were all God's idea in the first place.

In the Psalms we are told, "For you formed my inward parts; you knitted me together in my mother's womb. I praise you, for I am fearfully and wonderfully made. Wonderful are your works; my soul knows it very well" (Ps. 139:13–14 ESV).

We can only love someone to the extent that we know them. If we know someone a little bit, we can love them a little bit. Maybe this is why we don't feel very loved if we maintain a lot of superficial relationships. It's only when we get to really know someone that we can love them and be loved by them in a deep, meaningful way.

The same thing applies to our relationship with God. I know lots of people who prefer to keep their relationship with God at a fairly shallow level. Maybe they are afraid of being found out for who they are, warts and all. They maintain a nice, surface spirituality that looks okay at first glance but lacks vulnerability and authenticity.

It's disappointing to consider that perhaps one of the shallowest hours of our week is when we go to church. We hide behind routine greetings, friendly chatter, and donuts, and we rarely open ourselves to be known in a vulnerable way. In fact, folks would get downright uncomfortable if someone opened up honestly about their hopes and fears. It is a common trait that some superficial churches have one or two misfits who share openly, and people accept them because they are like "designated mourners" who grieve loudly so the rest don't have to.

God loves us because he knows us better than we know ourselves. King David wrote, "O Lord, you have searched me and known me! You know when I sit down and when I rise up; you discern my thoughts from afar. You search out my path and my lying down and are acquainted with all my ways. Even before a word is on my tongue, behold, O Lord, you know it altogether" (Ps. 139:1–4 ESV).

The love of God becomes connected to the implications of that love affecting our lives. I know I have been guilty of talking to people about God's love but then quickly jumping into the issues of our sin. Maybe, as a pastor, it seemed necessary to me to discuss sin—though only if it was their sin we were discussing, not my own. That wouldn't be much fun.

The implications of God's love are not focused on our sin at all. Rather, they focus on what the Lord wants to do in us and through us. He wants us to come alive in Christ and then to live in grace, forgiveness, and freedom as we become the new people he intended us to be.

Maybe it was simple insecurity; I'm not really sure. Over the years I have asked Christ to come into my life dozens of times. Lots of those conversion experiences happened when I was young, and they all were sincere as far as I knew. Looking back, I think whenever I messed up or things didn't work out the way I had hoped they would, I assumed it was because I hadn't gotten my conversion experience right. Otherwise, why would I be so messed up? Then I would try again, hoping this time it would work out and my life would be much better.

It was kind of like being caught in a spiritual version of the movie *Groundhog Day*—doomed to repeat the same day over and over until I got it right. It was very difficult to see myself as the new creation God intended, apart from my awareness of sin and failure, even though I knew I was forgiven and loved.

We all have perspectives that affect our self-image, worldview, and perception of the world around us. When Bobbi Reed and I teamed up to coauthor the book *Building Strong People*, we had very different perspectives. She was working as a warden of a state penitentiary and I was pastoring a church. I thought we had nothing in common, but I soon realized that being a penitentiary warden and pastoring a church were more similar than you might think.

Bobbi told me that in all the years she'd worked in the prison system, she'd never met a "guilty" inmate. No one ever admitted to being guilty of the crimes for which they were serving time. I was surprised when she told me this. Then I thought about heaven, where because of the grace, mercy, and love of God, there are also no guilty people. So maybe heaven and the California prison system are more similar than any of us thought. Evidently, neither place has any guilty people.

But more to the point, I began to realize that, as a pastor, I was doing things wrong. I tended to see my job as helping people get over their struggles. I tried to help them identify problems or difficulties and find ways to manage deficiencies. Of course, it didn't end there. I also tended to evaluate and judge people based on their particular set of problems, sins, shortcomings, or struggles. Once I figured out a person's weakness, I could categorize them and relate to them based on my stereotypes.

I knew that stereotyping people like this was a stupid thing to do, yet I still did it. I suppose when I could lump people together into categories, I believed I knew how to relate to them more easily based on their particular problem or circumstance. Of course I was wrong! The Bible tells us, "From now on we regard no one from a worldly point of view. Though we once regarded Christ in this way, we do so no longer" (2 Cor. 5:16).

My worldly point of view included viewing people in such a way that I could put them in a tidy mental box and relate to them accordingly. It made life easier for me, because I didn't have to deal with them as unique individuals whose lives, relationships, and issues were often complicated, thus making them hard to "fix"—but even more interesting and worth getting to know.

I have a hunch that many pastors and priests throughout history have done the same as I did, hearing confessions and counseling people in order to know everyone's struggles and problems. Then they could relate to folks based on stereotyping their problems. Of course, treating people in this way fails to grasp the significance of the truth, "if anyone is in Christ, the new creation has come: The old has gone, the new is here!" (v. 17).

Why is it so hard to recognize this powerful truth? Why is it difficult to treat people like they are a new creation? Why do I struggle to treat myself like a new creation? Too often we hold on to old, comfortable patterns, even when they no longer work for us. For example, when someone asks me about myself, my automatic response is to give a short list of negative things, most of which I dealt with in the past. Perhaps it would be more honest to share some good news about what new things God is doing in my life now!

It's Complicated

I've noticed on Facebook that under the category "Relationships," there are several options to choose from, such as, like married, single, divorced, or widowed. Turns out one of the most popular options that people choose is "it's complicated." Why is this the popular choice? Perhaps it's because relationships of any kind are complicated; it is hard to truly understand other people and know how to treat them in healthy, caring ways.

"You fight your superficiality, your shallowness," writes Philip Roth, so as to try to come at people without unreal expectations, without an overload of bias or hope or arrogance, as untankable as you can be. You come at them unmenacingly, on your own ten toes instead of tearing up the turf with your caterpillar treads. You take them on with an open mind as equals, and yet you never fail to get them wrong.

You might as well have the brain of a tank. You get them wrong before you meet them, while you are anticipating meeting them. You get them wrong while you're with them, and then you go home to tell somebody else about the meeting and you get them all wrong again.

Since the same generally goes for them with you, the whole thing is really a dazzling illusion empty of all perception, an astonishing farce of misperception, so ill equipped are we all to discover another's interior workings and invisible aims.[6]

Even with our best intentions, relationships can be fraught with misunderstanding and frustration. It is a common human trait to act stupid with the very people we care most about. And for those whom we don't care about, the stupidity goes off the charts. But it doesn't have to be this way.

We can stop being stupid when we begin to see people through the eyes of God's love. This probably isn't possible until we allow God's love to penetrate our own defenses and shape how we see ourselves.

By the way, it is easy for me to write about God's love for you. I'm convinced that his love is available for you and can bring change, healing, hope, and joy to your life. Yet for me, I'm not so sure. I find myself celebrating God's love for you while wrestling with the issue in my own life. You might think I'm being not so smart in struggling to realize God's love for me when I can quickly acknowledge it for others. Of course you would be right. And that is exactly why the message of the Bible is "God loves you—don't be stupid."

The proving ground for our faith seems to be the way we treat people in the world and in the relationships that form throughout our lives. On the one hand, we are called to certain personal character traits: "The fruit of the Spirit is love, joy, peace, forbearance, kindness, goodness, faithfulness, gentleness, and self-control. Against such things there is no law" (Gal. 5:22–23). Then the text shifts to warn us about certain relationship traits: "Let us not become conceited, provoking and envying each other" (v. 26).

We can have hope because we are not stuck without the possibility of tangible change, growth, and new beginnings. As God helps us become men and women of character, he also helps us relate to people in new, loving, and nonmanipulative ways. How we treat the people closest to us, how we relate to the world out there, and how we treat those who've struggled, fallen away, or are broken for whatever reason are a reflection of how we experience God's love in our own life.

11

The Power to Change

You can't let your past hold your future hostage. — LL Cool J

What makes it so difficult for us to make the changes we want and need? Every new year, and several times during the year, I resolve to make some changes that I think will improve my life. I know what I need to do and what I need to stop doing. I sometimes create a chart to keep track of my progress, and even enlist a few people to encourage me along the way. What could possibly go wrong?

I'd like to tell you what a great person I have become through all the changes I've made, but unfortunately my good intentions and sincere attempts have pretty much left me where I started. And evidently, I'm not the only one.

One study, for example, found that 90 percent of coronary bypass patients go back to their old, unhealthy eating habits within two years of their operation.[1] At one time I joined

Weight Watchers (now WW) and actually achieved my goal weight and was awarded the big brass key prize for lifetime achievement. And like most folks, I have also gained back all the weight I lost—and more.

This tendency toward failure applies to relationships, churches, and business settings as well. A 2014 Deloitte study of more than five thousand innovations over fifteen years calculated a success rate of only 4.5 percent. That means over 95 percent of the changes failed.[2] Certainly this is not a very impressive statistic.

Why do we so often fail to change? What makes it so difficult to succeed?

One obstacle to following through on desired changes is our basic misunderstanding of willpower. Thinking that we are stronger than we actually are leads us to underestimate how difficult it is to make changes in our lives. But good intentions and sheer willpower are not enough to bring success. If we depend on them and we fail, we feel even more like failures because we assume others have accomplished their goals solely by their willpower. There must be something wrong with us.

However, what if it isn't up to us to bring about the desired changes by our own strength? I believe there is freedom that comes when we can see ourselves as men and women on a journey. Our lives are a work in progress, and God is not finished with us yet.

Paul writes, "I do not consider myself yet to have taken hold of it. But one thing I do: Forgetting what is behind and straining toward what is ahead, I press on toward the goal" (Phil. 3:13–14), and he also writes, "[I am] confident of this, that he who began a good work in you will carry it on to completion until the day of Christ Jesus" (1:6).

It is very encouraging to realize that God has begun a good work in us. He hasn't given up on us, and he is at work to grow us into the men and women he always intended us to be. It isn't up to us to perfect ourselves. That's God's job—not ours. When we can see ourselves as a work in progress, it becomes easier to give others a break as well and recognize we are all imperfect fellow strugglers.

Inside and Out

There are two parts to every change we attempt. One part is our inner thoughts and intentions. The other is our overt actions. And we are not left alone to struggle and try to change on our own strength and willpower. "For it is God who works in you *to will* and *to act* in order to fulfill his good purpose" (Phil. 2:13, emphasis mine). Change requires not merely action nor simply willpower, but God's leading us in both our will and our actions.

Changes don't come about solely because of our inner intentions, processes, or convictions, because these must lead to tangible action for the desired changes to become established. Change happens when we take our inner goals and intentions, then look outward and start acting as if the change has already occurred.

We can start willing and doing instead of waiting for things to magically change. Rather than merely looking inward and trying to feel more loving about a person we care about, for example, we start doing what a loving person would do. If a loving person listens, then we put down the phone, turn off the TV, physically turn toward the other person, and listen to what they are saying. Possibly we take another step and ask appropriate questions to clarify what they are expressing.

Or, if we want to be more grateful, we don't settle for looking inward to seek a spirit or mood of gratitude. Instead, we think about what a grateful person would do, then we go to the store, buy a nice card, write a note of thanks and appreciation to someone, put a stamp on it, and mail it to them. If we start to do this, others will think of us as a kind, grateful person, and we will begin to see ourselves in that light.

Waiting until we feel a certain way inside, or until we have arrived at a place of confidence and good fortune, is a sure path to failure when it comes to making changes. The challenge is to link our actions and feelings together.

Big and Small

Sometimes we are blocked from making changes because we feel overwhelmed by the bigness of the challenges and our apparent insignificance. Many of us have a built-in mindset that assumes, since we are only one person with limited resources and abilities, we probably can't make a difference anyway—so why even bother.

I know I have felt this way. But only recently, I heard about ninety-nine-year-old Captain Tom Moore. Born in Yorkshire, England, Tom was a WWII veteran who'd moved in with his daughter and her family after his wife died. During the coronavirus pandemic, when the whole world was shut down by shelter-in-place mandates, he thought he might raise a little money by walking laps in the backyard and having friends and family make pledges to support him. It seemed like a fun way to get exercise, and he decided that any money donated would go to support the National Health Service Charities in England. He picked them, he said, because "our National Health Service is good—they do so much good for me—I had a broken hip and I had cancer and they treated me magnificently.

"I think people realize that . . . everyone, wherever they are, gets equally treated, just as well, with the same efficiency and kindness that we get from our nurses and doctors—who, after all, at the moment are on the firing line of the coronavirus crisis."[3]

When he started walking (using a walker for support), his daughter posted on the JustGiving fundraiser site that he would attempt to walk one hundred laps, hoping to raise perhaps as much as one thousand pounds. But less than a month later, when Captain Tom's one hundredth birthday came around, his inspiring efforts had captured hearts across the UK and raised over thirty-eight *million* pounds for charity. Prince William called him "a one-man fundraising machine!"[4] Now Captain Tom says he's thinking about doing another hundred laps and seeing if he can help charities even more.

While many of us sat around watching TV and complaining about not being able to do anything, Captain Tom energized many across his country to join together for a worthy cause. At one hundred years of age, he didn't have much, but he did have his walker, a small backyard, and a willingness to do what he could to make a difference in the world. I guess he makes all my excuses seem feeble.

Captain Tom's amazing accomplishment is a marvelous blend of getting an idea, taking action, and involving others for the purpose of helping make a difference. It only took a couple of months before the news came from Buckingham Palace that Queen Elizabeth II was going to knight Captain Tom and promote him to the rank of colonel in recognition of his extraordinary accomplishments for the good of the entire United Kingdom.

I guess all the usual excuses—like we're too old and we don't have the talent or money or whatever—go right out the window when we see what can happen if we try.

Loss and Gain

When asked, I used to jump in to help people make changes in their lives, or help churches and organizations change to meet new challenges. I also got involved with couples in counseling who expressed the desire to make changes in order to improve their relationships. Things seemed exciting at first and desired changes would start to occur, but then the positive energy would start to fade, people reverted to old patterns of behavior, and soon everyone was mad and wanted to go back to the old ways. It took a long time for me to realize what was happening and understand why it can be so difficult to change.

I finally realized all change is experienced by people as loss. If we don't recognize this, we'll forever wonder why we get close to the change we want but then it all falls apart. Whether it is change in individuals, relationships, or organizations, the reality is the same. Change causes us to feel a sense of loss, which then turns to anger. As the grief and anger grow, no one wants to be in conflict with themselves or others, so they revert back to how things were before the attempt to change occurred.

Because of this pattern, it often takes a long time, and a lot of failed attempts, to bring about lasting, positive change. People might talk about change as something needed, wanted, and even happily anticipated. Then as the change begins to occur, the pain of the inevitable loss begins to set in and anger starts to rise, and they will most likely swerve away from the pain of change in order to regain their old sense of stability.

In churches, for example, new pastors are often welcomed with enthusiasm as congregations celebrate the new energy and growth that will be experienced as a result of the pastor's leadership through the change process. Even when the congregation is clearly told that the changes to lead to growth will be difficult and will result in these feelings of loss and anger, they still excitedly embrace the idea of change. Of course, when people feel the loss and get angry, their feelings aren't aimed at the process but at the pastor who is making them feel this way. Inevitably, they storm after that new pastor like villagers attacking Frankenstein's monster, driving him or her away so they can seek another new pastor who will lead them through the changes.

In business, the change process is usually turned over to highly paid outside consultants. They lead the company through teambuilding, goal-setting, and mission-clarifying exercises until a vision statement is produced that clearly expresses the new goals and the necessary changes that must be made to accomplish them.

Of course, when the changes result in feelings of loss, as they inevitably will, anger surfaces and the changes are derailed, the plan set aside, and the outside consultant blamed. At least this system protects in-house management from blame and turns the anger toward the outsider rather than company leadership. Maybe if churches used outside consultants who could be blamed instead of their pastor, there might be less turnover of pastoral leadership?

And yet change can happen, in spite of the obstacles. "Christianity means change is possible," writes John Piper.

Deep, fundamental change. It is possible to become tenderhearted when once you were callous and insensitive. It is possible to stop being dominated by bitterness and anger. It is possible to become a loving person no matter what your background has been.[5]

He goes on to point out that God is the decisive factor in making us what we can be, and thus it is not up to us in our own strength to simply decide we want to be different. For change to occur, God will be leading and empowering us throughout the process. With wonderful bluntness, the Bible says, "Put away malice and be tenderhearted" (see Eph. 4:31–32). It does not say, "If you can," or "If your parents were tenderhearted to you," or "If you weren't terribly wronged or abused." It says, "Be tenderhearted."

Appearances and Integrity

Authentic change is possible when we stop fretting over superficial issues and allow the Lord to restore us from the inside out. We can be free from worrying about what others think about us and free from the temptation to please people. Seeking approval from others is a sure way to keep up appearances while we ignore the vital work of living a life of integrity. Sometimes appearances become more important to us than who we really are.

I grew up in a family that went through a period of several years during which we were supposed to be very concerned about what the neighbors thought of us. I didn't know much about why it mattered, or why my parents seemed so concerned about it. However, I learned at an early age how to use this to my benefit. If, for example, I'd been naughty and was getting spanked (which did seem to happen quite a bit), I figured out that screaming and yelling my head off at the first swat would create a huge ruckus.

Sometimes I'd yell so loudly that Lindy Palucha and her parents would hear me, and they would come running from their house next door, wondering what terrible disaster had befallen me. With every spank, my parents would be yelling, "Shut up! Be quiet!" But I wasn't going to stop screaming because I knew rescue was on the way. I knew my parents did not want the neighbors to come, see me getting spanked, and return home thinking badly of us.

Caring so much about what others might think of us affected our family in many ways. Instead of figuring out what we thought, who we were, or what we might do in different situations, we'd simply look around at our neighbors and try to be more like them. Of course, we never bothered to realize the neighbors were struggling with their own problems and were trying to keep their image up just like us.

This superficial covering-up carried over into most areas of life. And today, we can use words like "peer pressure" and "crowd mentality" to describe our actions. These actions occur when good-hearted people get together with a group of others and start to do crazy things. When asked about it, we'll often just say something like, "Well, the crowd influenced me, and I was pulled along in the momentum like being swept away in the river current."

But the integrity that Christ brings to our lives means we are free from peer pressure or crowd mentality or worrying about what the neighbors might think.

No little attempts to mask our problems will suffice. We need Christ. We need the kind of tangible change that results in personal *integrity*, which is a great word and an even better reality.

Integrity occurs when all the parts are working together and holding together so that there is stability and a sure sense that *this is what is meant to be*. Integrity leads us to be authentic and transparent. The opposite of integrity is maintaining the appearance of having it together, which unfortunately I've spent a lot of time trying to cultivate, as if I could fool people into thinking I was stable.

A while ago, on a dreary, rainy day in Seattle (of course this could describe any day of the year), I stepped out the second-floor door onto our deck that provided a beautiful view of the Puget Sound. However, it took me only about five seconds to realize something was wrong. The deck had dropped down about five feet, angling away from the house. Thinking to myself, *This can't be good*, I called my friend Dave and asked him to help me do a quick fix so the neighbors wouldn't know that our deck was collapsing—was, in fact, completely rotten.

With Dave's helpful ingenuity and tools, we propped up the deck using a car jack and some boards. He warned me that even though it looked fine, I shouldn't let anyone walk out on it because of the very good chance the whole thing would come crashing down at any minute. I told him I wasn't ready to replace the rotten deck, I just wanted to buy a little more time. He looked at me like I was crazy and told me several times that he would happily replace the old deck and maybe save someone's life in the process.

I thanked him for his help and good advice, which I didn't act on until about a year later, as I was standing on that old, propped-up deck and felt it beginning to sway under my feet. I should have realized that old decks, like our personal lives, can come crashing down. When there is no integrity, the only thing left is disintegration. Falling apart.

My deck was disintegrating even though it looked fine from the street. In the same way, our lives can be falling apart but people don't notice because we've propped up our emotions and actions with the equivalent of a car jack and a few boards. I finally had to admit my deck desperately needed integrity, not more paint.

I called another friend, Daniel, who came to check things out. Without even asking, he immediately tore down the deck, pointing out to me that almost every beam and post was completely rotten. "You could have died up there, if a wind came up off the water." I thought that seemed a little melodramatic—until he started poking holes right through the beams using a fork. That got my attention.

Daniel proceeded to build a new deck for me that was twice as large, didn't sag or sway, and wasn't held in place by a car jack. When he was finished building the new, sturdy deck, he stood on it with me and said, "This now has integrity!"

Jesus entered into our world and enters into our lives, establishing integrity in who we are. How we appear on the outside now is in harmony with what's happening inside, and our purposes and goals line up with our actions and behaviors. We aren't undermining ourselves or betraying ourselves or others. And our focus is true, because we are clear all the way through with no cloudiness or illusions. As we let Jesus have more control of our lives, we experience greater integrity without the risk of disintegrating.

Who we are, regardless of the people around us, is significant because our character is developed and shaped by the freeing power of God's love.

————

When my dad died, I went to San Diego for his memorial service and participated alongside family members and friends as we celebrated his life and remembered him from our unique perspectives and experiences. When the official services were over, our family gathered at my brother Richard's house. He hosted us because he was the oldest of us four kids and would probably be the next one to go, as I reminded him.

I was sitting in a small study, apart from the big gathering, when my nephew Thomas walked in with a handful of stuff he wanted to show me. "I was looking around Grandpa's garage," he said, "and I picked out things to remember him now that he's gone." It was mostly little scraps of paper with handwritten notes Dad had stashed away in drawers. Then Thomas handed me a small notebook that had page after page of things my father had written to himself. I recognized his precise civil engineer's handwriting as I turned the pages. On about the fourth page, he had written, "Always remember, stature not status."

After growing up in our family, where it seemed there was a preoccupation with worrying what the neighbors might think of us, I was surprised to discover my dad had already determined there was a better way to live. I don't recall ever having a conversation with him about that, nor had he overtly mentioned this that I remembered. Thomas and I sat and talked about how my dad must have written the note just for himself, to remind him later in life not to get his priorities messed up. Evidently, he wanted to remember that who he was as a person, a follower of Jesus, a husband and father, and a contributor in the community had nothing to do with what others might have thought, wanted, or expected from him and had everything to do with being a man of stature and integrity, uncluttered by comparison or evaluations from other people.

Called by Name

Not only are we free from worrying about what the neighbors may or may not be thinking, we're also free to discover who God made us to be with all our quirks, uniqueness, and possibilities. We don't need to try to be like others. We aren't like robots coming off an assembly line. There is no need to struggle to try to fit in, because God intentionally made each of us unique, different from everybody else. With Christ in our lives giving us integrity, we become more ourselves, more unique, and more free than we ever imagined.

"One of the most unfortunate aspects of our culture," writes psychologist Ty Colbert,

> is that we start out all too willing to affirm a newborn child's uniqueness and creativity, only to squash this same person later as he develops his unique identity. When the child is young, we feel free to affirm him without hesitation. We are amused with his silliness, his spontaneity, and his off-the-wall remarks. We enjoy the ways he is different from other children. But when that child begins to grow up, stretch his talents, challenge our values, and compete with us, his identity begins to threaten us. As he grows and develops, we—as parents, as a society and often as a church—find it necessary to imprison him in our opinions of who and what he should become. When we do that, we give him the message that he's not okay. We take from him the cornerstone of his own selfhood, the right to be okay with himself.[6]

Another powerful motivator of positive change is recognizing and affirming the unique qualities and giftedness of ourselves and others. Such affirmation is powerful perhaps because it is so rarely given. Parents don't want to "spoil" a child, teachers don't want them to get "swelled heads," and coworkers don't want them to "think they are better than they are."

In children, the fear of failure is often connected to the fear of being abandoned. This results in a tendency to overestimate the risk being taken and imagine the worst possible scenario: being abandoned physically or emotionally. Unless combatted with the truth, these fears stay with us as we mature and lead to us convincing ourselves that we shouldn't even try to change, believing it probably won't work out anyway.

Self-image isn't based on how we see ourselves, nor is it based on how others see us. Our self-image is formed by *how we think* others see us. These ideas are formed and reinforced through the years. Our perceptions can form from seemingly harmless input. Something as small as nicknames we might have been given as children can shape our reactions and relationships for years. Perhaps you were "the pretty one" or "the smart one." Or perhaps you were Dummy, Clumsy, or, like the kid in *Leave It to Beaver*, you were "Lumpy." As children, these names may have seemed harmless to us, yet they have a way of sticking and following us throughout our lives. "Pencil-neck geek" was a phrase used by a pro wrestler on those phony Saturday "wrasslin" shows we used to watch, and soon we were using it to put down kids we didn't like. Even a president of the United States became famous for his habit of shaming and belittling opponents by labeling them with nicknames reminiscent of a schoolyard bully. Names can be a powerful way to hurt and belittle those around us.

Jesus understood the importance of names and often chose to call people by a new name as he went about his earthly ministry. To Simon, the volatile disciple who appeared to have mood swings, was impulsive, and even had violent outbursts, Jesus gave the name Peter, which meant "rock." Peter's new name described him as a solid, consistent person who could be trusted and relied upon. Later Saul, a persecutor of the young church, encountered Jesus on the road to Damascus and was given a new name, Paul, a missionary and defender of the faith. There may be nothing more powerful than setting aside old attitudes toward people and identifying new traits or characteristics that can become identifying marks of both who they are and who they are becoming. Names mattered in the Bible, and the power in a new name was also understood. "The nations will see your vindication," Isaiah writes, "and all kings your glory; you will be called by a new name that the mouth of the LORD will bestow" (Isa. 62:2).

There's a village on the island of Anglesey, Wales, that may have one of the longest names ever bestowed on a place. It is the community of Llanfairpwllgwyngyllgogerychwyrndrobwllllantysiliogogogoch. Now, I don't speak Welsh, but I understand the name means "The Church of Saint Mary in a hollow of white hazel, near to the rapid whirlpool, and to Stitisilio Church near to a red cave."

Evidently, the inhabitants realized the importance of giving their village a name that would be an accurate description for all who came to visit. And here I thought Albuquerque was a long name.

Names are powerful descriptors that can serve to bless or curse a person. When we use names that call out the strengths, abilities, and positive character traits of a person, it is a significant gift of affirmation.

Positive affirmations are actually expressions of gratitude. When we affirm a colleague by communicating positive aspects we have observed, it expresses gratefulness not only for their traits but also for the person. One of the most impactful affirmations involves transforming seemingly negative traits and reclaiming them as positive characteristics. When we are well aware of our shortcomings and failures, it is all the more necessary to be reminded of who we are and how needed we are, just the way we are.

I've always been aware that I had a lot of problems. As a young pastor, I had the lurking fear of being "found out." I kept thinking if people realized what I was really like, they wouldn't want me to be their pastor. I had come to believe the subtle message that God couldn't use me unless I changed and became someone else. The way I was and all the things I wasn't kept me feeling outside and alone.

One day, I was nervous waiting outside the door to interview for a church staff position. I wanted to make a good impression while appearing capable and creative, but I knew that if I didn't tell them of my problem fitting in to the "pastor" mold, they would find out sooner or later. Tired of pretending, during the interview I decided that I would rather not work in a church where I couldn't be myself. It was time to be real.

I began to tell my story, sharing my strengths as well as my frustrations in ministry. I told of my struggles to fit in and how I was often unpredictable and impulsive in both my work and my relationships. I even confessed that I wasn't super spiritual, that I was rather undisciplined in my devotional life, and, even worse, my office tended to look like a bomb just went off in it. I let them know that I was serious about my relationship with Christ but that I wasn't very religious in the sense of wanting to maintain religious traditions I found meaningless or forms of worship that felt stilted to me. Hymns had their place, but I really preferred rock and roll.

About halfway through the interview, the senior pastor, Bruce Larson, stopped me. "It seems to me you are one of those people who color outside the lines," he said. I felt myself getting tense at being found out. *Guess I'll need to look for a different job now; maybe I'm not cut out to be a pastor.* "That can be a spiritual gift," Bruce continued, "one that the church desperately needs. I think we've suffered from stereotypes in the pastoral role for too long."

Could he be right? I had been found out as someone who didn't quite fit the mold, but instead of being told to change in order to be acceptable, I was being affirmed for who I was. Those quirks of personality and temperament that I assumed had to be hidden away could instead be seen as gifts to be used by God for his purposes. In that one conversation, the circle of affirmation and inclusion had been drawn around me, and I was released to be myself. It forever changed my life.

We all know what it's like to be in a relationship with someone who doesn't like us the way we are. There are endless pressures to change, spoken and unspoken, in order to be more acceptable to them. There is also great loneliness because we know we'll never be acceptable even if we do try to change.

I'm grateful God doesn't play that game with us. He embraces us as we are, complete with strengths and flaws, hopes and fears, gifts and warts. He invites us to be ourselves in relationship with him. He only asks us to trust him with every area of our lives. He already knows us better than anyone else, and he loves us regardless. Thus our relationship is grounded in reality and demonstrated in personal integrity.

Plan Your Past Today

The future isn't what it used to be. — Yogi Berra

Most of us spend a lot of time and energy planning for the future. That makes perfect sense, doesn't it? But why don't we put just as much energy into planning our past? Think about it. If I want to someday look at my life and think about my past experiences, adventures, friendships, and accomplishments, what will I need to do now so that the memories I'll have will be the ones I want to remember?

Rather than allow the past to creep into our present-day thoughts and feelings, it would be far better to reverse the process and use today to shape our memories and feelings from now on. Even though we don't usually think about the past we are creating today, each day we have a chance to intentionally shape our past.

To plan our past is not a complicated nor particularly difficult thing to do. It involves just a few steps and a bit of creativity.

1. *Look back.* Think back to a time when you were able to
   use your talents, skills, and gifts. What were you doing?
   Did you find something you didn't know you were good
   at? What did you put off that you wished you'd spent
   more time on?

2. *Clearly see the present.* What impact are you making
   now? Is this enough for you? What do you think created your present circumstance? What did you enjoy
   doing in the past, but now the joy is waning? What are
   you clinging to that used to define you, but now you
   are thinking it is time to let go? What do you feel you
   should have done by this time in your life? What is stopping you?

3. *Explore your new story.* If you had the opportunity to
   express your talents, what could you accomplish? What
   do you dare to dream of doing? What do you long to
   experience or create? Is there something you are called
   to do but you think it's impossible? Could someone
   help you?

4. *Leave behind.* To step into your potential, what do you
   have to leave behind? What can you say no to now?
   What can you cross off your to-do list to give yourself
   more time and energy to spend on what is most important now?

5. *Plan your steps.* Create a way to remember your intentions, so when next year rolls around, answering these
   questions will be easier.

To effectively make a change, start small with something that isn't really that big of a deal but might help you do something just a little bit better than before. This might include small steps such as doing something around the house without being asked. Perhaps it's taking an extra ten minutes each day to just be with yourself, or it's talking with a loved one about something on your mind or on theirs. Maybe it's talking back to one negative thought you have each day.

Predictably Unpredictable

While the past can give some insight into possible changes, as well as help us understand how or why things may have become the way they are today, there are some things it can't do. It can't tell you what to do to change things right here and now.

People who are a lot smarter than you and I have tried and failed to predict the future. Thomas Watson, the president of IBM during the dawn of the computer industry, famously predicted, "I think there is a world market for maybe five computers."[1] This brilliant insight was only slightly more wrong than that of Ken Olsen, founder of Digital Equipment Corporation, who emphatically stated, "There is no reason anyone would want a computer in their home."[2] It was less than four years later when the IBM PC was launched, proving that predicting the future is not all that easy. But how do we plan in a world where the future is uncertain?

Rather than fight against or fear uncertainty, we can factor uncertainty into our planning process. Today, uncertainty and randomness are big influencers that help determine success and failure. New social networks catch on, a random video goes viral, and it is difficult to know what the next big influencer will be. Social influence can move in random ways, usually quite quickly, which in turn makes predictions and forecasts pretty much useless. Traditional ideas of identifying who are experts and influencers are no longer accurate. Even the concept of trusting science and so-called experts is being challenged.

The *Wall Street Journal* analyzed twenty-five thousand user contributions at six large sharing-and-collaboration websites. What they found was that a very small number of participants commanded extremely high levels of influence. Of Netscape's million-plus users at the time, for instance, 13 percent of the postings rated "most popular" came from a single user. Of the nine hundred thousand users of Digg, a third of the contributions rating highly enough to make it to the home page came from just thirty people. The researchers then decided to track down one of Reddit's most widely read users, a blogger named Adam Fuhrer, in order to figure out why his opinions on software and legal issues had been so widely praised by other users. What they found was that Adam was twelve years old and lived with his parents in Toronto![3]

If we wanted to predict the next Adam Fuhrer, it would be a completely impossible task. But knowing that technology, networks, and social influencing make our world less predictable is a kind of prediction in itself. Planning in our uncertain world requires us to be flexible. We prepare for several different outcomes. Rather than trying to make the one big guess as to what might happen, we make multiple guesses. We place many small bets on a variety of options. We stay flexible and agile.

The planning strategies we may have been taught in the past are almost completely irrelevant today, because our teachers assumed our future was predictable. We were taught to forecast the future and also predict how to have a happy and successful life in it. Then the next step was to come up with a number of possible scenarios for achieving that life. After considering various strategies to get us where we wanted to go, we were to simply pick the best one to be our goal. Finally, we could figure out what we would need to get there, like education, money, a spouse, and so on. Then we could head out and do it. It was as simple as that, and if we failed along the way, it was probably because we didn't plan well enough or weren't clear about our goal.

While this planning model may work in a predictable world with a predictable future, it can turn into a complete failure when things can't be predicted and the future is uncertain. But just because we can't simply imagine a perfect job for ourselves since our future isn't predictable doesn't mean we should drift aimlessly and avoid any planning. We simply need to be smart and recognize that our approach to planning needs to be different.

Instead of picturing the perfect job or career and developing steps to get there, we can start with a general direction based on our interests and skills that we want to move toward. Then we develop strategies to find or make opportunities that match our interests and skills. Rather than searching for the perfect job, we create it either within an existing organization or on our own.

I spent many years working with long-range planning committees, most of which saw their task as coming up with goals and plans to help the organizations become what they anticipated they'd need to be in five or ten years. Looking back, I don't think any of the planning teams succeeded in anticipating what was ahead for them, and nearly every long-range plan was rendered irrelevant.

It's impossible to predict what things will be like in five or ten years. Change happens quickly, and the ways we work and function will be very different in the foreseeable future.

177

While the future may be changing rapidly, there are some things we can know with certainty. The first is Jesus's promise to never leave us nor forsake us (see Heb. 13:5). This means that, even in the midst of uncertainty, we are never alone. The Lord who knows us, made us, and calls us by name is with us in every circumstance.

The second thing we can know is what's important and valuable to us. What matters to you? What are the unique gifts and abilities you have to offer? Do you want to travel? Is there a particular industry that interests you? Are you willing to move frequently to have new responsibilities, or would you rather put down roots? How you answer these and other questions can help point you in positive directions.

The *Seattle Times* ran a story about a shoeshine man in downtown Seattle who lived out his values in surprising ways. "It takes special skills to be a shoeshine man," writes Nicole Brodeur.

> Not only do you have to buff away the scuffs of the streets, you have to smooth clients' rattled nerves. Listen. Nod along. Leon McLaughlin, 53, has been doing that for more than a decade at Seattle's Columbia Tower—all the while keeping his mind on a bigger problem. Today he and members of World Vision will travel to Bolivia to see the installation of water-filtration machines in 10 hospitals and 10 schools. . . .
>
> "There is such a need," McLaughlin said. "Two million children are dying a year. 1.2 billion people are hurting from waterborne illnesses. We have to bring that number down to zero." [4]

It all started for McLaughlin when he met a woman in Mexico who told him a story that changed his life. She mentioned that an American tourist once asked to use her bathroom. While he was in there, he drained all the water from her tub, thinking he was doing her a favor. She began to cry. It was all the water she had for the month.

McLaughlin was moved to try to help. After taking some classes on water system repairs over the internet, he formed a company to bring water filtration machines to developing countries. His first success was the installation of a filtration machine in Bolivia that required no electricity and could be assembled without complicated instructions or special tools. It generated 740 gallons of clean water per hour. That was years ago—and McLaughlin has not faltered in his mission.[5]

Whenever he's back at his shoeshine stand, McLaughlin gets advice from customers—and gives it. Money people, businesspeople, and lawyers give him free counsel along with the cost of the shine, and in return McLaughlin shows them the potential for saving lives. "We can let the world know that we have all these children dying, this situation is urgent."[6]

It is easy to take people for granted and not realize that we all can apply our passions and abilities to make a difference and express our deepest values and beliefs. Mr. McLaughlin lives his values whether he is traveling internationally to make a difference in children's lives or shining shoes in downtown Seattle.

Plan for Purpose

We can start a new past today. When we consider our abilities and uniqueness and the needs and opportunities around us, we begin a process that has the potential to energize us and make a difference for others. When Rick Warren wrote *The Purpose Driven Life*, for example, his words encouraged people with a reminder that when we live in harmony with our life purpose, the whole world is transformed.

Now, I confess I'm not very good at planning. Okay, let me try again: I'm a terrible planner. Fortunately, all through my life I've been near people who can and do make plans. Along the way, I've even taken credit for some of their great plans. Don't get me wrong; I'm not against making plans, I just don't do it very well. So I got to thinking, *What would planning look like for those of us who are "planning challenged"?*

It is perfectly fine to start with small steps and let the process pick up momentum. Big things are accomplished with small steps in the right direction. The first step is to consider your desire. What do you want? What do you want to happen? What do you care about? What would be fun to do? What needs your involvement? The Bible tells us God wants to give us the desires of our hearts (see Ps. 37:4). Perhaps it's time to ask ourselves what that desire is, or at least what it might be.

Then it's time to make a list of what you're naturally good at, what you'd rather avoid, and the types of conditions that make you thrive—or not. You probably have a pretty good idea to start with, plus there are many good assessment tools to help with this, such as Gallup's Strengthsfinder 2.0, which is designed to help you recognize strengths and talents you might have, and the Myers-Briggs test, which can help you see how preferences and behaviors can motivate or frustrate you.

Ask yourself what inspires and motivates you. Think about some of your experiences in terms of what accomplishments you are most proud of, or what you are doing when you shine most brightly. These can help identify some of your top values.

There are a couple of ways to approach identifying our desire. The first begins with self-examination. What do we enjoy doing? What are we good at? What are some needs we have that we could leverage to also help others with similar issues? What problems or difficulties have we dealt with that could help us relate with people who are experiencing similar problems? How might our gifts and our struggles be used to help someone else? The second approach to identifying our desire involves looking outward at the world around us and focusing on an issue, problem, or opportunity that needs to be addressed. Leon McLaughlin was touched when he heard a woman in Mexico share her struggle. Singer Bob Dylan would spread newspapers all over the floor then sit on the floor and look for articles about people and situations he might address in song.

We too can scan news articles to see what catches our attention. Perhaps there is a need in your community or a problem you could help resolve. There may be a ministry or community effort that needs volunteers. Not all opportunities are problem based, though. There may be an exciting community project or celebration coming up that could use your experience and assistance in planning and implementing for it to be successful, for instance.

Small Steps

Once we've explored possibilities for where we could get involved in doing something we care about, it's time to take a small step toward it. Many times people think they have to take a monumental leap into the deep end of the pool in order to make a difference. Too often it is such a big step that we end up backing away and not doing anything because it seems overwhelming.

By taking a small step, we put our idea into action without setting ourselves up for burnout and frustration. Small steps are encouraging, because they provide an opportunity to act while getting involved a little at a time. If, after taking a small step, we decide to pursue something different, there is no sense of guilt or failure that we've let people down.

After taking a small step, it's important to evaluate your experience. Success or failure or something in between—consider what you may have learned from taking that step. There is much to be learned every day. You may have learned more about the cause or issue you addressed. Perhaps you learned that it is more complicated than people might think it is.

You may have learned that you have a lot to offer, and that your abilities are just what are needed at this time. Perhaps you learned from your experience that there are things you might do differently, or there may be better ways to address the need. You might even learn that it would be more fun and effective if you invited a friend to join you so you can approach it from a team perspective.

After considering what you learned from that first small step, it's time to take another step. This is an important part of the process, because we are able to use the things we learned from taking that first step and move forward in a meaningful way. "Progress is made when we risk taking a small step, consider what we learned from the experience, then take another small step forward."[7]

These actions help overcome our natural tendency to quit after the first step. Again, the next step needn't be a huge action agenda, merely another small step, which is followed by considering what we learned from the second step. It may seem insignificant to make small steps followed by identifying what we have learned, but it leads to great success.

While President Jimmy Carter was working as a peanut farmer in Georgia, he heard about the lack of decent housing available for families in need. Rather than simply writing a check to a good cause, he put on his tool belt and volunteered one afternoon at a local building site of Habitat for Humanity. He enjoyed pounding nails and sawing boards, and it got him out in the fresh air working alongside other volunteers.

That first small step was the beginning of a lifelong passion to use his hammer, his resources, and his influence to help families realize their dream of safe, clean housing. Even during his years in the White House, he would visit worksites and volunteer to make a difference.

One step at a time, dreams are fulfilled. The steps we take today become the past we remember tomorrow.

13

Renewed Mind = Transformed Life

What is so fascinating and frustrating and great about life is that you're constantly starting over, all the time, and I love that. — Billy Crystal

I have a confession to make: I play golf excessively. Don't worry, I'm not very good at it, but I do love to play the game. Recently I played in a Pro-Am event at our home course, which is a tournament where PGA golf professionals are teamed up with everyday people like me. I was really nervous at first, but after a while my nervousness went away—because it was overwhelmed by frustration and shame directly related to my horrendous playing.

About halfway through the round, the pro golfer who was in our group quietly took me aside and asked if I would like him to give me a few tips that might help my game. I was desperate by this time, so I eagerly anticipated whatever help I could get from him.

He told me that he had been watching me play, and he thought my stance was good, I was balanced pretty well, my grip on the club was very good, and he liked the way I took the club back and swung through the ball. Then he looked straight into my eyes and said, "I'm concerned about your head."

I thought of all the things we are supposed to remember about our head during a swing, like keep your head down, don't move it back and forth, stay level, and be sure to keep your head from bobbing up and down. So, I asked him if he thought I was moving my head around when I swung at the ball. "I don't know about that," he said. "I wasn't watching you that closely. I'm wondering what is *in* your head!"

My first thought was, *You're a golf pro, not a psychiatrist*, but I kept quiet and just smiled a little. He continued, "I'm just wondering what's in your head, like with this next shot, what do you see when you think about hitting the ball?"

"Oh, that's easy," I told him. First, I described the trees near me and how the limbs extended out over the fairway, interfering with my shot. They would require me to keep the ball low so it didn't get up into the branches. Then I told him of the trees on the other side of the fairway that were dense and very hard to get out of if I hit over there. Of course, ahead were a couple of sand traps, which are scary to me (since they are called "hazards" in golf lingo). I really wanted to avoid going in those because I'd probably have a terrible time trying to get out of the sand. Then there's that hill up ahead, and past the sand was the beverage cart, so I need to not hit into that.

"That's your problem; you've just named every negative thing that could possibly happen to ruin your shot," the pro said. "What's in your head is keeping you from playing your best golf. It's like your head is filled with fear and irrational hopes." I told him of course I saw all the negatives. That's the way I looked at life: I focused on the obstacles and setbacks while at the same time I longed to suddenly start playing really well.

"It may work in the rest of your life, but it's not going to help your golf game," he said. "All you need to do is think about where you want the ball to go, and then hit it! Swing freely. Take the club back and swing as freely as you can. Don't even think about anything else, just where you want the ball to go, that's all! Oh, and you might try smiling."

Wow, here I was, going along obsessing about everything, being my usual negative self, and this golf pro figures out that my head is messed up. And he wants to take all the memories and hurts and pains that I've carried with me and free me from that. All so I can play freely.

Could it be that the secret to living like there's no yesterday comes down to being "transformed by the renewing of your mind" (Rom. 12:2)? Maybe it's as simple as that golf pro asking me, "What's in your head?" Maybe if we want to grow, we'll have to start with changing how we think.

Renewing Our Thoughts

My Grandma Ruth was a wonderful lady who raised my dad and my aunt as a single mother after her husband died from a botched surgery. She was full of Eastern European wisdom and pithy sayings. Once when I was a kid and was complaining about how I was being mistreated by my brothers and generally not appreciated by everyone else, she knelt down and looked me in the eye to share some of her wisdom. I fully expected her to remind me what a fine grandson I was and how I didn't need my brothers because I was quite all right just the way I was. After all, what grandmother wouldn't affirm a little kid?

Instead, she looked at me intently and said, "Johnny, when you have limburger cheese on your nose, the whole world stinks!" Then she walked away, leaving me to ponder the wisdom of the ages.

Where do we begin to change our patterns of thinking? One starting place is to talk back to your unhealthy inner statements. Just because we might think something, doesn't mean that thought gets the final word. With practice, we can stand up to our negative thoughts and tell them they are wrong.

When you find yourself thinking, *This will never work out; it's going to be a big disaster!*, challenge the assumption by reminding yourself of times your efforts weren't a disaster. Change the thought to, *It may end up a disaster, but it doesn't have to. There were times I tried my best and it worked out well. I'm going to give it my best effort.*

Not everything we tell ourselves is true. Sometimes our minds lie to us. It is necessary to challenge the lie. When you tell yourself you can never lose the extra weight, or you'll never get the job you want, or no one will ever love you, challenge the lie. Whenever you fight back and challenge the lies, it trains your mind to begin to see yourself in a different way.

It is easy to fall into unhealthy patterns of thinking, which is why mind renewal is so important. In the same way that physical exercise builds up our muscles and helps keep us physically strong and agile, mental exercise keeps our minds sharp and positive, able to resist unhealthy patterns of thinking.

Take a chance by stepping up. It's easy to hold back and wait for someone to notice you, but don't let insecurity or fear keep you sidelined. You can set goals and plan next steps, use social media, network with friends, and start implementing your ideas. After all, they are yours, and you don't need the approval of others to get started.

"One of the most notable characteristics of worrying is it fragments our lives," writes Henri Nouwen.

> The many things to do, to think about, to plan for, the many people to remember to visit, to talk with, the many causes to attack or defend, all these pull us apart and make us lose our center. Worrying causes us to be all over the place but seldom at home.
>
> One way to express the spiritual crisis of our time is to say that most of us have an address but cannot be found there. We know where we belong but we keep being pulled away in many directions as if we were homeless. All these other things keep demanding our attention. They lead us so far from home that we eventually forget our true address—the place where we can be addressed.[1]

When life has pulled us this way and that, when we are finally tired of being tired, when we have tried and failed to feel satisfied, it's time for renewal in our minds. I've spent a large part of my life being restless and unsatisfied. I've chased dreams, problems, people, and sometimes problem people. Like most things, this probably started early for me.

189

Hope and Fear

There were two things in my early life instrumental in shaping me into becoming the person I am. First, *Why Johnny Can't Read* was my early reading textbook, and I thought it had been published just for me to help me with my problems. I used to wonder how they knew I couldn't read. Did my mother call the publisher and tell them? I resolved never to have to read books about what I could or couldn't do. I also learned how to read eventually, which shaped my life in more ways than I'll ever know.

The second shaper of my life was seeing The Rolling Stones in one of their first American concerts. I couldn't get a date, so I took my little sister, Florence, which turned out to be a big mistake—*huge*. I think the opening groups were Paul Revere and the Raiders and The Turtles. Then, suddenly, The Stones were on stage. I was spellbound as Mick hugged the microphone while Keith buzz-sawed his way through the opening notes, and then Mick started singing about not being able to get any satisfaction! Like with my reading textbook, I assumed the song was written just for me, because it was just how I felt in my young brain.

As it turned out, my kid sister hated the music. Then she got theological and had the realization that if Jesus returned to earth at that moment, we would be left behind because we were listening to that "evil rock and roll." When I ignored her demands to leave, she pulled on my shirt so hard it ripped off my body, leaving me to wonder why God invented families in the first place.

Now, looking back, I'm quite aware that my young brain was practicing the mental distortion of *personalization*. I took both influences very personally, believing they were about me and for me. Which almost certainly wasn't true, but that didn't matter, because it was the start of a lifetime quest trying to find satisfaction. Perhaps I could have combined those two influences and called it, "Why Johnny Can't Get No Satisfaction!" Sometimes my efforts to find satisfaction led me to exciting and joyful experiences, and other times they led to lonely, empty places.

The renewing of our minds involves two important issues that affect all of us: hope and fear. Unmet longings haunt us with hopes unfulfilled. When one longing is met, more rise up to take its place, causing us to experience emptiness in the midst of abundance. We can feel lonely in a crowd, like a failure in the midst of accolades, and insecure and misunderstood while in committed relationships.

There can be a sense that we may be missing out, making it nearly impossible to be grateful in our current situations. The Bible provides a long history of our attempts to be more, have more, and get more, to the extent that we strive to obtain instead of accepting that God wants to give us the desires of our hearts as a free gift of grace.

Like so many characters in the Bible, we fill our lives with strenuous efforts to earn attention, make something happen, and even try to help God fulfill his promises. In fact, we do everything humanly possible to avoid accepting the free gift of grace.

Adam and Eve were not content being merely the creation of God. They wanted to be God. They were unsatisfied with only knowing the good; they also wanted to have a knowledge of evil in order to know what God knew.

Cain wanted God's attention and acceptance on his own terms, and he murdered his brother when his disobedience was revealed. Abraham didn't believe that God would fulfill his promise of a child for him and his wife, Sarah, so he fathered an illegitimate son to try to fulfill God's promise through his own human efforts.

Jacob wanted more, so he schemed with his mother to deceive his father and cheat his brother by stealing the family inheritance. Moses couldn't wait to see the deliverance of his people, so he murdered a man and was exiled for many years. King David was restless and unsatisfied, so he committed adultery and murder to gain the love and attention he thought he deserved.

The prophet Elijah felt afraid and depressed and wanted to commit suicide to ease the pain he was experiencing. Judas couldn't understand why Jesus wasn't performing to his expectations, so he betrayed him to his death, perhaps hoping it would force the Lord to establish his kingdom on earth.

> The history of humanity is a history of everyday people who take matters into their own hands. They are afraid to trust God. They refuse to step out in faith into the uncharted waters of tomorrow. They are desperately willing to do anything or try anything—anything but receive the grace that restlessly pursues us.[2]

Fear may be the greatest obstacle in all of life. It underlies much of our personal and social dysfunction and keeps us from experiencing the transformed life God intends for us. Fear keeps us from intimacy by leading us to hold back, pretend, lie, and conceal our true selves so that we don't live with transparency, vulnerability, and authenticity.

Fear of others causes us to become defensive, wary, and sometimes disengaged from people whom we perceive as different from us. Rather than seeking engagement and connection, we'll put up walls of protection that serve to isolate us and keep us from embracing the world that Jesus entered and loved.

When our son, Damian, was in middle school, we traveled to Greece. Being a precocious kid, he had become fascinated with the work of Nikos Kazantzakis, including the film *Zorba the Greek*. In anticipation of visiting the island of Crete, which had been Kazantzakis's home, Damian bought a T-shirt with a bold quotation from Kazantzakis. Since the quotation was in Greek, I didn't know what it said, but it was just a T-shirt so I gave it no thought.

After touring the ancient island, we ended up in a crowded marketplace, perusing shops and looking for souvenirs. Suddenly an elderly Cretan ran up to Damian and pointed his finger at his chest while yelling at him. I rushed over to defend my boy, but Damian let me know he could handle the situation. I watched as he looked the old man in the face and, nodding his head, said, "Yes, I do." At this the man beamed a smile where there was once a threatening glare, and said to Damian, "Good." Then he walked off into the crowd without another word.

I asked Damian what that was all about, and he explained that the man pointing at his T-shirt was asking, "Do you believe what this says?" Realizing that I had no idea what the quotation on his shirt said, Damian rolled his eyes as if I was an innocent child who must have the simplest things explained.

It said, "I hope for nothing. I fear nothing. I am free."

Then he told me it was the epitaph on Nikos Kazantzakis's gravestone. To which he added, "I guess they take Kazantzakis seriously on Crete."

What if this revered and sometimes controversial Greek author was on to something? What if the hopes and fears that limit us are keeping us from experiencing the freedom in which we were meant to live? Perhaps the renewing of our minds that leads to transformed lives is simply letting go of our fiercely pursued unmet longings and surrendering our fears that imprison us. Then we too may be free.

The character in the Bible whom I think embodies all the worst of unfettered hopes and longings blended with fear is Jacob, the conniver, cheater, betrayer, and all-around con man. Toward the end of his life, he hears that his estranged brother, Esau, is coming for him with a huge entourage and army, presumably to take revenge for the evil and pain Jacob had caused him.

Jacob was terrified when he heard he was about to come face-to-face with his brother, whom he had cheated, abused, robbed, and shamed. In his typical manipulating way, he devised a plan to distract his brother so he could possibly gain the upper hand if there was to be a fight to the death. Several times he sent extravagant gifts to Esau, telling the gift bearers to make sure they told him they were from Jacob.

When the brothers finally met, "Esau ran to meet him and embraced him and fell on his neck and kissed him, and they wept" (Gen. 33:4 ESV). Then Esau asked what was the meaning of all the company he'd met on the road. Jacob admitted he'd sent them so he might find favor. Then Esau said, "I have enough, my brother; keep what you have for yourself" (v. 9 ESV).

Anger, fear, and bitterness all grow where there is an absence of gratitude. Perhaps our minds will experience renewal and our lives will be transformed as we choose to be grateful in every situation and in every problem. We don't have to be thankful for everything, as that would be masochistic, but we can be thankful in every circumstance. When we choose to be grateful and to let go of our fears, it opens the door for forgiveness, reconciliation, contentment, fearless courage, and authenticity.

Notes

Chapter 1 What If There Was No Yesterday?

1. *The Lion King*, directed by Roger Allers and Rob Minkoff (Burbank, CA: Walt Disney Studios, 1994), DVD.

Chapter 2 Fuhgeddaboudit! There's No Future in the Past

1. Bruce Larson, *Living beyond Fear* (New York: HarperCollins, 1990), 27.
2. C. S. Lewis, *The Voyage of the Dawn Treader* (New York: HarperCollins, 1997), 64.

Chapter 3 It's All about Freedom

1. Frederick Buechner, "Morality," August 8, 2018, *Frederick Buechner*, https://www.frederickbuechner.com/quote-of-the-day/2018/8/8/morality?rq=morality.
2. Gordon MacKenzie, *Orbiting the Giant Hairball* (New York: Viking/Penguin, 1998), 33.
3. Paul Tournier, *Guilt and Grace* (New York: Harper, 1962), 119–20.
4. Philip Yancey, Facebook post, April 17, 2019, https://www.facebook.com/PhilipYancey/posts/2412756255435510.
5. Barry Schwartz, "More Isn't Always Better," *Harvard Business Review* (June 2006), https://hbr.org/2006/06/more-isnt-always-better.
6. Barry Schwartz, *Paradox of Choice: Why More Is Less* (New York: Harper Perennial, 2005), 2.
7. Brian Vandenberg, "Magical Thinking," *Britannica*, accessed November 5, 2020, https://www.britannica.com/science/magical-thinking.
8. Viktor Frankl, as quoted in Neel Burton, "Man's Search for Meaning," *Psychology Today*, May 24, 2012, https://www.psychologytoday.com/us/blog/hide-and-seek/201205/mans-search-meaning.

Chapter 4 The Power of (Positive/Negative) Thinking

1. As quoted in "The World According to Garp by John Irving—Under Toad—," *thingsthatmadeanimpression*, July 28, 2013, https://thingsthatmade animpression.wordpress.com/2013/07/28/excerpt-from-the-world-according -to-garp-by-john-irving-under-toad/.

2. Abraham Maslow, *Motivation and Personality* (New York: Harper, 1954), 86.

3. Rebecca A. Ferrer et al., "Unrealistic Optimism Is Associated with Subclinical Atherosclerosis," *Health Psychology* 31, no. 6 (November 2012): 815–20.

4. Geoff Chen, "How Negative Visualization Can Change Your Life (Premeditatio Malorum)," *The Stoic Sage*, February 9, 2020, https://thestoicsage .com/premeditatio-malorum-the-art-of-negative-visualization/.

5. As quoted by Julian Sancton, "Woody Allen on Death: 'I'm Strongly Against It,'" *Vanity Fair*, May 15, 2010, https://www.vanityfair.com/holly wood/2010/05/woody-allen-on-death-im-strongly-against-it.

6. Sarah Elizabeth Adler, "The Power of Negative Thinking," *Atlantic*, January/February 2018, https://www.theatlantic.com/magazine/archive/2018 /01/the-power-of-negativity/546560/. See also Frieder R. Lang et al., "Forecasting Life Satisfaction Across Adulthood: Benefits of Seeing a Dark Future?" *Psychology and Aging* 1 (March 2013): 249–61.

Chapter 5 Binocular Vision—Seeing with 20/20 Distortion

1. Steven Stosny, "The Key to Having an Adult Relationship," *Psychology Today*, May 23, 2018, https://www.psychologytoday.com/us/blog/anger-in -the-age-entitlement/201805/the-key-having-adult-relationship.

2. *Lost in Translation*, directed by Sofia Coppola (Los Angeles: Universal Pictures Home Entertainment, 2004), DVD.

3. Douglas Coupland, *Life After God* (New York: Simon & Schuster, 2002), 285.

4. Stosny, "Key to Having an Adult Relationship."

5. Tim Chaves, "How Black-and-White Thinking Can Kill Your Business," *Forbes*, April 4, 2018, https://www.forbes.com/sites/theyec/2018/04/04/how -black-and-white-thinking-can-kill-your-business/#597186a2fe0f.

6. Ryan Martin, "What Is Overgeneralizing?" *Psychology Today*, August 1, 2019, https://www.psychologytoday.com/us/blog/all-the-rage/201908/what -is-overgeneralizing.

Chapter 6 How to Make Yourself Miserable

1. As quoted in "C S Lewis: Hell", *Quite A Quote!*, September 4, 2018, http://quiteaquote.in/2018/09/04/c-s-lewis-hell/.

2. C. S. Lewis, *The Great Divorce* (repr., New York: HarperCollins, 2001), 11–12.

3. As quoted in "53 Insightful Dwight D. Eisenhower Quotes That Are Timeless," *The Famous People*, accessed November 5, 2020, https://quotes .thefamouspeople.com/dwight-d-eisenhower-1270.php.

4. Wayne Dyer, as quoted in Preston Ni, "How to Stop Blaming Others, and Be Free and Powerful!" *Psychology Today*, November 2, 2014, https:// www.psychologytoday.com/us/blog/communication-success/201411/how -stop-blaming-others-and-be-free-and-powerful.

5. "The Insufferable Need to Always Be Right," Exploring Your Mind, August 4, 2017, https://exploringyourmind.com/insufferable-need-always-right/.

6. George Bernard Shaw, as quoted by ForbesQuotes, accessed October 5, 2020, https://www.forbes.com/quotes/3370/.

7. Daily Mail Reporter, "My Mother Abandoned Me When I Was Just Eight: Hugh Jackman's Secret Heartache," *Daily Mail*, October 24, 2012, https://www.dailymail.co.uk/tvshowbiz/article-2222597/Hugh-Jackman-My -mother-abandoned-I-just-eight.html.

Chapter 7 Why Am I Worrying about Worrying?

1. "Corrie ten Boom Quotes," Goodreads, accessed September 30, 2020, https://www.goodreads.com/quotes/110765-worrying-is-carrying-tomorrow -s-load-with-today-s-strength--carrying-two.

2. Quoted in Claire Gillespie, "7 Silent Signs of High-Functioning Anxiety," The Healthy, updated October 20, 2020, https://www.thehealthy.com /mental-health/anxiety/high-functioning-anxiety/.

3. Carina Wolff, "Signs of a High-Functioning Anxiety Disorder," Bustle, February 17, 2017, https://www.bustle.com/p/11-signs-you-might-have -a-high-functioning-anxiety-disorder-dont-even-realize-it-38777.

4. Jeffrey Bernstein, "Four Magic Words to Overcome Anxiety," *Psychology Today*, March 16, 2014, https://www.psychologytoday.com/us/blog /liking-the-child-you-love/201403/four-magic-words-overcome-anxiety.

Chapter 8 Living beyond Past Trauma

1. Jeanette Settembre, "Abigail Breslin Talks to Moneyish," MarketWatch, May 8, 2018, https://www.marketwatch.com/amp/story/guid/8253f215-6adb -4bab-bf12-40f5bc8218c4.

2. Settembre, "Abigail Breslin Talks to Moneyish."

3. Judith Lewis Herman, *Trauma and Recovery* (New York: Basic Books, 1997), 35.

4. Herman, *Trauma and Recovery*, 35.

5. As quoted in Caroline Rogers, "Mister Rogers Quotes That Remind Us All to Be Good Neighbors," *Southern Living*, August 8, 2018, https://www .southernliving.com/culture/mr-rogers-quotes.

6. Brennan Manning, *Ragamuffin Gospel* (Portland, OR: Multnomah, 2000), 11.

7. "Anderson Cooper Tries Schizophrenia Simulator," YouTube video, 5:04, uploaded by HLN, June 11, 2014, https://www.youtube.com/watch?v=3qEPz6EepNA.

8. Bessel van der Kolk, "Bessel van der Kolk: Restoring Joy and Treating Traumatic Stress," Byron Clinic, accessed October 5, 2020, https://byronclinic.com/bessel-van-der-kolk-restoring-joy-trauma/.

Chapter 9 It Takes Ten "Atta-Boys" to Make Up for Every "You Jerk"

1. Allie Caren, "Why We Often Remember the Bad Better than the Good," *Washington Post*, November 1, 2018, https://www.washingtonpost.com/science/2018/11/01/why-we-often-remember-bad-better-than-good/.

2. *The Simpsons*, season 11, episode 1, "Beyond Blunderdome," directed by Steven Dean Moore, aired September 26, 1999, on Fox Network.

3. Caren, "Why We Often Remember the Bad Better than the Good."

4. Kevin Hart, *I Can't Make This Up* (New York: Simon & Schuster, 2017), 167–68.

5. Daniel Kahneman and Amos Tversky, "Choices, Values, and Frames," *American Psychologist* 39, no. 4 (1984): 341–50.

6. Kahneman and Tversky, "Choices, Values, and Frames."

7. Centre for Confidence and Well-Being, "The Negative Brain," Positive Psychology Resources, accessed October 5, 2020, http://www.centreforconfidence.co.uk/pp/overview.php?p=c2lkPTEmdGlkPTAmaWQ9NDU=.

8. Rick Hanson, "The Practical Neuroscience of Happiness," *Greater Good* (podcast), UC Berkeley, September 22, 2010, https://greatergood.berkeley.edu/article/item/the_neuroscience_of_happiness.

9. Hanson, "Practical Neuroscience of Happiness."

10. Charles Schwab, as quoted by Henrik Edberg, "34 Inspiring Quotes on Criticism (and How to Handle It)," *The Positivity Blog*, April 20, 2020, https://www.positivityblog.com/quotes-on-criticism/.

11. Tony Campolo, speaking at Colonial Church of Edina, Minnesota, November 9, 2007.

Chapter 10 What We Need to Know to Live Like There's No Yesterday

1. Joe Johnson, "Top 10 Darwin Award Winners Ever," Babble Top, October 14, 2017, https://babbletop.com/top-10-darwin-award-winners-ever/.

2. Rupert Taylor, "Stupid People Don't Know They Are Stupid," Owlcation, February 21, 2020, https://owlcation.com/social-sciences/Stupid-People-Dont-Know-They-Are-Stupid.

3. Taylor, "Stupid People Don't Know They Are Stupid."

4. Oscar Wilde, "The Critic as Artist Quotes," Goodreads, accessed October 7, 2020, https://www.goodreads.com/work/quotes/579364-the-critic-as-artist.

5. C. S. Lewis, *The Lion, the Witch and the Wardrobe* in *The Chronicles of Narnia* omnibus edition (New York: HarperCollins, 2004), 146.

6. Philip Roth, *An American Pastoral* (New York: Houghton Mifflin, 1997), 35.

Chapter 11 The Power to Change

1. Jeff Wise, "How Real Life Change Happens," *Psychology Today*, March 19, 2013, https://www.psychologytoday.com/us/blog/extreme-fear/201303/how-real -life-change-happens.

2. David A. Shore, "Making Change Happen: Five Keys to Driving Successful Change Initiatives," *Harvard Extension School Professional Development Blog*, accessed October 7, 2020, https://blog.dce.harvard.edu/professional -development/making-change-happen-five-keys-driving-successful-change -initiatives.

3. Sara Spary, "Captain Tom Moore, 99, Says He Is 'Overwhelmed' by Raising $23 Million for the NHS," *CNN World*, April 17, 2020, https:// www.cnn.com/2020/04/17/uk/captain-tom-moore-raises-23million-scli-intl -gbr/index.html.

4. "100-Year-Old Captain Tom Moore Hoped His Charity Walk Would Raise $1200. It's Soared to about $40 Million," *CBS News*, April 30, 2020, https://www.cbsnews.com/news/captain-tom-moore-birthday-charity-walk -coronavirus-40-million-dollars/.

5. John Piper, "You Are Not Enslaved to Your Past," Desiring God, October 12, 2015, https://www.desiringgod.org/articles/you-are-not-enslaved -to-your-past.

6. Ty Colbert, *Why Do I Feel Guilty When I've Done Nothing Wrong?* (Nashville: Thomas Nelson, 1993), 12.

Chapter 12 Plan Your Past Today

1. Robert Strohmeyer, "The 7 Worst Tech Predictions of All Time," *PCWorld*, December 31, 2008, https://www.pcworld.com/article/155984 /worst_tech_predictions.html.

2. Strohmeyer, "The 7 Worst Tech Predictions of All Time."

3. Don Peppers, "6 Strategies for Dealing with Uncertainty in Business," *Fast Company*, March 13, 2012, https://www.fastcompany.com/1824457 /6-strategies-dealing-uncertainty-business.

4. Nicole Brodeur, "Shoeshine Man on a Mission," *Seattle Times*, September 9, 2008, https://www.seattletimes.com/seattle-news/shoeshine-man -on-a-mission/.

5. Brodeur, "Shoeshine Man on a Mission."

6. Eric Johnson, "Eric's Heroes: Leon McLaughlin, the Shoe-Shine Guy," *Komo News*, December 7, 2016, https://komonews.com/news/erics-heroes /erics-heroes-leon-mclaughlin-the-shoe-shine-guy.

7. Leonard A. Schlesinger, Charles F. Kiefer, with Paul B. Brown, *Just Start: Take Action, Embrace Uncertainty, and Create the Future* (Cambridge, MA: Harvard Business Review Press, 2012), 14.

Chapter 13 Renewed Mind = Transformed Life

1. Henri Nouwen, *Making All Things New: An Invitation to the Spiritual Life* (repr., New York: HarperOne, 2009), 65.

2. John F. Westfall, *Enough Is Enough: Grace for the Restless Heart* (Grand Rapids: Zondervan, 1993), 164.

John F. Westfall is founding pastor of Harbor Church in the Pacific Northwest. A former radio show host, an ordained pastor, an adjunct professor at Fuller Theological Seminary, and a popular retreat and conference speaker, John is the author of *Getting Past What You'll Never Get Over*. He lives in the Seattle area with his wife, Eileen.

Connect with
JOHN F.
WESTFALL

JohnFWestfall.com

Sometimes you can't just
pick yourself up and move on.

But even then, THERE IS HOPE.

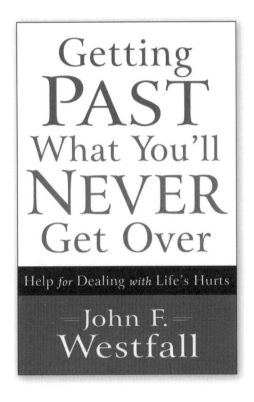

With deep compassion, John F. Westfall leads you beyond
your pain and into a life of confidence, freedom, and secure
joy. You may carry the wounds of the past, but that doesn't
need to keep you from living a hope-filled future.